BE A CHANGEMAKER

HOW TO START SOMETHING THAT MATTERS

Laurie Ann Thompson

SIMON PULSE
New York London Toronto Sydney New Delhi

BEYOND WORDS
Hillsboro, Oregon

An imprint of Simon & Schuster
Children's Publishing Division
1230 Avenue of the Americas
New York, NY 10020

20827 N.W. Cornell Road, Suite 500
Hillsboro, Oregon 97124-9808
503-531-8700 / 503-531-8773 fax
www.beyondword.com

This Beyond Words/Simon Pulse edition September 2014
Text copyright © 2014 by Laurie Ann Thompson
Illustrations copyright © 2014 by iStockphoto.com
Cover photograph copyright © 2014 by iStockphoto.com

For information about special discounts for bulk purchases, please contact
Simon & Schuster Special Sales at 1-866-506-1949 or business@simonandschuster.com.

The Simon & Schuster Speakers Bureau can bring authors to your live event.
For more information or to book an event contact the Simon & Schuster Speakers Bureau at
1-866-248-3049 or visit our website at www.simonspeakers.com.

Managing Editor: Lindsay S. Brown
Editors: Nicole Geiger, Ali McCart, Emmalisa Sparrow
Copyeditor: Ashley Van Winkle
Proofreader: Michelle Blair
Interior and cover design: Sara E. Blum
The text of this book was set in Adobe Garamond Pro and Interstate.

Manufactured in the United States of America

10 9 8 7 6

Library of Congress Cataloging-in-Publication Data

Thompson, Laurie Ann.
    Be a changemaker : how to start something that matters / Laurie Ann Thompson.
    pages   cm
    Includes bibliographical references.
    1. Social action—Juvenile literature. 2. Community development—Juvenile
        literature. 3. Community leadership—Juvenile literature. 4. Political
        participation—Juvenile literature. I. Title.
HN18.3.T46 2014
361.2—dc23
                                                                2013044580

ISBN 978-1-58270-465-4 (hc)
ISBN 978-1-58270-464-7 (pbk)
ISBN 978-1-4814-0169-2 (eBook)

TO MY FAMILY,
FOR THEIR ENTREPRENEURIAL SPIRITS
AND UNFAILING SUPPORT

Contents

Foreword

BE A CHANGEMAKER—NOW

Don't wait.

Don't wait to be powerful, to change the lives and communities around you significantly.

There is nothing like it. Once you discover that you can visualize the next step society should take, and then you discover that you can lead others to turn your vision into reality, you can do anything.

The only way to know you are a changemaker is to be one—and the younger, the better. If you change your world in middle or high school, you will change it again and again throughout your life. (Almost all the social entrepreneurs I know had such early practice.) You can do so by creating a tutoring service, or radio program, or business, or whatever turns you on. Once you have made your dream work, and its value is apparent, others will keep it going after you have moved on.

Becoming a changemaker is quite like getting on a bicycle and mastering its zen. Except it is far, far more important and requires far more practice. Laurie Ann Thompson's book will help you get started. Laurie shows how everything starts with asking yourself, "What's my passion?" Once you find your passion and apply it to a problem you care enough to do something about, then you are on your way! Laurie's stories beautifully illustrate how everyone—and really we mean *everyone*—can create powerful change in the world.

Indeed in another ten or so years there will be very, very few opportunities for anyone who is not a changemaker. Artificial intelligence, algorithms, and the web are fast stripping away jobs of intellectual, not just physical, repetition. Already that includes, for example, almost half of what architects used to do and probably three quarters of archeologists' work of exploration.

Instead, as the rate and pervasiveness of change continue to accelerate exponentially (a mathematical fact), we will all be valued more and more in terms of how well we envision and enable others to move to better futures.

If you are to contribute, let alone lead, in this "everything changing, everyone a changemaker" world, you need to begin writing your story now.

As you launch your venture, you will master the most critical skills you will need in life: (1) applied empathy (deeply understanding all the people and groups around you so you will do as much good and as little harm as possible), (2) teamwork, (3) new leadership (very different dimensions when everyone is a changemaker!), and (4) changemaking (envisioning and engineering better futures). These skills are so rich and so subtle that mastery comes only with persistent, intensive, real engagement, and practice.

By the time you become an adult, you will know in your heart whether or not you are powerful, whether or not you are a changemaker—and whether or not you have mastered the underlying skills. This core self-understanding will define your role in life and how you relate to others.

What is the key to making your first, life-defining commitment to changing your world? Just give yourself permission. Many will tell you that you cannot. Please ignore them—but do so politely, gently: for those whose lives are limited because they never gave themselves permission, your stepping out stirs regret. That is what you are hearing.

Far better to listen to your own imagination.

Bill Drayton
Founder of Ashoka, an organization
that finds and supports changemakers

It's Your Turn Now

Change will not come if we wait for some other person or if we wait for some other time. We are the ones we've been waiting for. We are the change that we seek.

Barack Obama, 44th President of the United States of America, in a speech to his supporters in Chicago on February 5, 2008

You've heard the saying, "If you want something done right, you have to do it yourself." I've found this to be true more often than one might expect. Sometimes it's because other people can't do it. They just don't have the skills or the tools that you do. Other times they just won't do it. It is, after all, what *you* want, and it's your definition of *right*.

How many times have you complained about something but done nothing to fix it? Or noticed something and thought, *Someone should do something about that*? We all have those thoughts sometimes. And it's okay, because none of us can solve every problem we encounter. But guess what . . . you're someone. And when you set your mind to it, you absolutely can do something that matters.

Fortunately, there are some exciting changes happening in your world right now. People are realizing that applying the best practices from the business world to the worst problems we face as a society is an effective step toward creating the solutions we need. And, modern-day technology makes it easier for everyone to do, especially young people. You truly have the power—now more than ever before—to be the change that you seek.

Profile
FREE THE CHILDREN

Craig Kielburger was flipping through the newspaper in search of comics when he came across the headline, "Battled Child Labour, Boy, 12, Murdered!" Because Craig was also twelve, the words grabbed his attention and he stopped to read the article. He soon learned that the boy, Iqbal Masih from Pakistan, had been sold into slavery at the age of four and chained to a carpet loom for nearly six years. After escaping, Iqbal spoke publicly against the common practice of child labor in his country and others. Many suspected Iqbal's death was an attempt to silence him and his message.

Craig had never heard of child labor, so later that day he did some research. What he learned shocked him: more than 250 million children were working around the world, many in slave-like conditions. It was more than Craig, growing up in a middle-class neighborhood in Ontario, Canada, could even imagine. So he decided to do something about it.

Craig went to school and told his class what he had learned. When he asked if anyone would help him stop child labor, eleven friends raised their hands. Together they embarked on a journey, founding a group called Free the Children. In his book, also called *Free the Children*, Craig says, "None of us had much experience with social justice work—just a desire to take action." As you'll soon see, that desire is enough.

At first, Craig and his friends had a hard time getting anyone to take them seriously. They approached several established charities to ask how they could help, but none of them were interested. What could a group of kids do about such a huge, complex problem? Finally they decided they would have to do it themselves.

After years of hard work and determination, Free the Children has grown and expanded. Now a respected international charity, educational partner, and leader in the field of youth empowerment, the group addresses all kinds of social issues in addition to child labor. Since 1995, Free the Children has provided:

- Medical supplies worth more than $16 million around the world

- Clean water, health care, and sanitation for one million people

- We Day events to celebrate youth activism and volunteerism, attended annually by 160 thousand teens

- Daily education for fifty-five thousand children

- Economic self-sufficiency for thirty thousand women

- Quality activities for millions of young people

- Construction of more than 650 schools and schoolrooms

- Programming and building projects in forty-five countries

So, what can young people do? Anything they set their minds to. And if they can do it, so can you.

WHY YOUTH?

Just like Craig (and in no small part thanks to Craig) more and more people—young and old alike—are realizing that young people really can make a big difference in their communities, in their countries, and around the world. It's called youth empowerment, and many people think it's the next big movement.

Like other movements before it—civil rights, feminism, and gay rights, to name a few—this new movement is about empowering a group of people whose opinions and abilities have previously been ignored by society. But this time, it's about empowering the world's youth—about helping people like you seize the power to make your world be everything you want it to be. And you can be a part of it.

In the past, movements mostly involved people waving signs, participating in marches, and banding together for rallies and protests: actions intended to force the people in power to do things differently. Those are still valuable ways to change the world, but today's activists have more options. Young people everywhere are rising up and directly creating the changes they want to see in their communities and around the world—right now. They're applying modern business practices and using powerful new technologies to build brand-new organizations from the ground up. They're solving the problems they see in the world around them—all by themselves. They are changemakers, and you can be one, too.

WHY YOU?

In case changing the world into what you want it to be and being part of the youth empowerment movement aren't enough for you, trying your hand at changemaking has other benefits, too. You'll learn more about something that interests you, find out more about yourself, have fun with your friends (and make new ones), and solve real problems. Launching a social venture—a project that seeks to fix a social problem—gives you experience being creative yet organized, working with a team, managing your time wisely, and setting goals and taking action on them—all skills that are critical to success in school, on the job, and in life.

Today's companies—more than ever before—are on the lookout for employees with proven problem-solving abilities, creativity, critical thinking skills, collaboration experience, and communication techniques. After becoming a changemaker, your resumé will practically write itself! Because of that, colleges and universities are looking for applicants who have these kinds of activities, too. Want something to show the college admissions officers—not to mention scholarship selection committees—that you stand out from the other applicants? Changemaking shows off your real-world leadership skills and demonstrates a commitment to community service in a way that short-term volunteer positions can't.

With all that to gain, what have you got to lose?

In My Experience

If someone had told me when I was a teenager that I could change the world, I think I would have laughed. I was female, at a time when that still limited my choices. I was short. I wasn't beautiful, wealthy, or connected to anyone with significant power or influence. I knew I wouldn't go to an Ivy League university. I had never led anything. In fact, I did my best to blend in and avoid being noticed at all costs. Change the world—me? Not likely.

Skip forward several years—okay decades—and I can only pity the girl I was then. That girl never knew I'd have a successful career working at IBM, Microsoft, and Intel—some of the biggest technology corporations in the world—or that I'd help launch a successful startup. She never guessed the satisfaction I'd get from volunteering for organizations whose missions I care about deeply. She couldn't imagine that I would find my true calling and become a confident leader in the process. And she couldn't have dreamed I would discover my path to changing the world.

I don't want you to have to wait that long. I want you to have all of those things—the sooner, the better—because I know you can dream it, and those dreams can come true.

YOU CAN DO IT

Maybe you think this sounds like something for *other* people—ones with money, IQ, connections, confidence, free time ... whatever? Think again. Everyone can be a changemaker! And that includes you. As Craig wrote for Santa Clara University's Architects of Peace project, "I realize, now, that each of us has the power to be Superman and to help rid the world of its worst evils—poverty, loneliness, and exploitation."

You already have the ideas, the passion, the energy, and the talent! You will have to learn a few new skills—basic tools that will help you get the job done. And, you'll have to work hard and do things you've never done before. But inside this book, you'll find all the practical knowledge as well as the encouragement you need to go out and truly make a difference.

Each chapter will introduce you to young people who have already changed the world. You'll see what they did, why they did it, and how they succeeded—or failed—so you can learn valuable lessons from their experiences. You'll also gain a whole lot of knowledge and find many resources to help you do it yourself. Plus, you'll discover some of the many existing organizations dedicated to helping people just like you.

Some of this information might seem a little overwhelming at first, but just take it in small doses if you need to, and work your way through it at your own pace. You don't even need to read this whole book before you start something that matters! You can read it cover to cover before you begin, or just start whenever you're ready and use this book as a reference along the way.

It's true that changing the world—even a small part of it—is rarely easy. You might not end up accomplishing what you set out to do, or it might take longer than you expected. But don't let that stop you! You can start creating the world you want to live in—today, tomorrow, and beyond—anytime you choose. You don't have to do it all, and you don't have to do it immediately. Just start something small, and see where it takes you. As Craig says in *Free the Children*, "It all begins when one person finds the courage to take action."

You are the changemakers and the change. I've seen it, I believe it, and I know it to be true.

Monique Coleman, actress, founder and CEO of GimmeMo.com,
speaking at We Day Seattle on March 27, 2013,
attended by the author

2

What's a Changemaker, Anyway?

How wonderful it is that nobody need wait a single moment before starting to improve the world.

Anne Frank, author, in *The Diary of a Young Girl*

I f our society is to continue to evolve and address the many problems we face, we must have more changemakers in all corners of the world who can and will take the initiative to create positive social change in their communities. Some of these changemakers will be social entrepreneurs, people who challenge the status quo with radically new and different ideas and then bring their visions to life to improve the world. Anyone, from anywhere, can become a changemaker or social entrepreneur. You can do it, too, just like Divine Bradley did.

Profile

TEAM REVOLUTION

Divine Bradley was no goody two-shoes. Growing up, he often felt the allure of life on the gang-infested streets of his Brooklyn neighborhood. Then, when Divine was seventeen, a close friend of his was murdered over a basketball game. That was Divine's wake-up call.

The kids in his neighborhood needed a safe place to hang out after school, but there weren't many options. Divine decided to create his own after-school program. But just getting the kids off the streets wasn't enough. Divine wanted to build confidence, teach leadership skills, and inspire a sense of community participation, too. He wanted to give young people positive role models and offer them a new direction. He wanted to change lives.

In 2000, Divine shared his idea with some neighborhood friends, and Team Revolution was born. The team started meeting on street corners, then moved to Divine's front porch, and then took over his family's basement. By 2002 the group had grown too big to fit in the basement anymore. Team Revolution needed its own space.

Could inner-city teenagers find a way to pay rent on a commercial space—legally? They weren't sure, but they decided to try. They got a $500 grant from Youth Venture, and within two weeks, they had raised close to $25,000—by selling candy! They secured their own space, and soon the members of Team Revolution had turned an idea into a safe, gang-free community center, complete with a movie theater, a recording studio, and administrative space.

That didn't necessarily mean happily ever after, though. "Getting everyone to believe that I was someone who was capable of doing something great, something positive, was a huge challenge," Divine told HowStuffWorks.com. So he worked hard to demonstrate results, forge strong partnerships, and build an organization that would last. Since then, Team Revolution has impacted thousands of young people in New York City and beyond and is a model for community centers around the world.

Through his work with Team Revolution, Divine himself became what he originally wanted: a positive role model in the community. He's now using his passions on an even larger scale and continuing to inspire youth as a Dream Director with The Future Project. Now that's what I call a happy ending.

CHANGEMAKERS AND SOCIAL ENTREPRENEURS

Divine Bradley is a great example of a changemaker. Divine didn't start Team Revolution to make money for himself. He just wanted to provide a safe, fun place for the neighborhood youth to hang out. Still, he had to find money, manage it carefully, and continue finding more in order to keep the community center running. Learning how to run a business helped Divine keep Team Revolution going strong for more than ten years.

Consider some of the businesses and organizations you're familiar with. Many, like Apple or Walmart, follow a for-profit business model. Their main goal is to maximize profit for their shareholders. Others, like the Red Cross or the United Way, are charities. They focus on collecting donations so they can redistribute the money and provide services to those in need.

Today's changemakers often fall somewhere in the middle—not entirely for profit or simply charitable. They use effective business practices to change the world for the better. Some of their organizations, such as Free the Children and Team Revolution, may be charities or nonprofits—spending most of their energy fundraising and then using that money to help solve a problem. Others, such as TOMS Shoes, may be for-profit businesses, selling a product or service to make money, but running their companies according to a core set of values and donating a significant portion of their profits to charity. In these cases, the leaders know that doing good and making money are not mutually exclusive. In fact, combining those two elements helps them succeed by creating a sustainable organization that people grow to trust and respect.

11

Some people get hung up before even starting any kind of venture because they think they need to decide right away whether it's a nonprofit charity or a for-profit business. They either don't know which one makes the most sense for their unique idea or are uncomfortable with going down a certain path. Because for-profit businesses exist primarily to make money, sometimes people think of them as evil or bad. Conversely, they might think of all nonprofits as good because their main goals are altruistic. In reality, it's just not that simple. Businesses can solve social problems and act responsibly while making a profit. And, of course, nonprofits can be wasteful, irresponsible, or even downright fraudulent.

You don't need to decide whether you want to start a charity or a for-profit business right now. In fact, your project doesn't even have to be a real business yet. For now, you can simply be a group of people working together to solve a problem, just like Team Revolution was when it first started out. The only thing your venture needs to do is make something good in the world. And the only thing you need to know to make that happen is that you are a changemaker. After all, as Divine's motto says, "The best way to predict the future is to create it."

Social entrepreneurship is changemaking taken one giant step forward to actually change the way the world works. It isn't just doing a good deed, nor is it running a successful business. It isn't a charity that asks people for money and then gives it all away, nor is it a business that is 100 percent focused on profit at all costs. Social entrepreneurs invent brand-new ways of getting things done and implement their visions throughout a society. As Bill Drayton puts it in his book, *Leading Social Entrepreneurs Changing the World*, "Social entrepreneurs are not content just to give a fish or teach how to fish. They will not rest until they have revolutionized the fishing industry." Social entrepreneurship is a growing movement that's changing the world for the better. The best way to become a social entrepreneur is to practice being a changemaker when you are young.

You've probably heard of other changemakers and social entrepreneurs and what they've accomplished, even if you didn't know that's what they are called. Let's think about where you may have encountered change-making and social entrepreneurship in your own life.

---

1. Think of famous people you've learned about who changed the world for the better. Perhaps you think of Mahatma Gandhi for his nonviolent approach to achieving social change. Or maybe you think of Steve Jobs because of the empowering technology he helped bring about. The people on your list might be historical or more recent.

2. Now, consider people in your community who started something that matters. Did a teacher at your school volunteer to lead an after-school activity? Did a government official launch a campaign to change citizens' behavior? Who organized the 5K your uncle ran in last November that raised money for cancer research? Each of these people could be considered a changemaker. Maybe they founded programs you or someone you know has benefitted from, or perhaps it was just something you heard about or saw advertised.

3. Think about your friends and classmates at school. Have any of them organized something that didn't exist before? Have any of them already made their marks on the world? They're changemakers, too!

4. How about your family? Do any of them run their own businesses or nonprofit organizations? Do they use business skills and procedures to do good in the world? You could easily be related to a change-maker or even a social entrepreneur. If none come to mind right away, ask your family members if they can think of anyone. Many of us have ancestors who were changemakers.

Did you notice how many different kinds of people popped into your mind during this exercise? That just goes to show that anyone can be a changemaker. It doesn't matter what race you are or whether you're rich or poor, a genius (or not), male or female, good-looking (or less so), outgoing or introverted, straight or gay, old or young, or anything else.

In My Experience

I never considered myself to be a leader. I was a shy, quiet introvert who hated public speaking, avoided arguments, and tried not to state an opinion. Then, the two leaders of my regional Society for Children's Book Writers and Illustrators (SCBWI) announced they were both stepping down. Someone needed to step up and assume the leadership roles, or the organization would shut down. It was a daunting role. At the time, the organization served almost a thousand people, put on more than a dozen events every year, and had a six-figure annual operating budget—it was all way out of my league. But no one else stepped up.

I was already working on this book when that happened. I'd volunteered in various roles for several different organizations. I'd been a manager at a major technology company, and I'd helped found an internet startup. But I had never done anything even close to what leading the SCBWI chapter would entail. It was way outside my comfort zone. But then it hit me: How could I write a book encouraging you to go out and be a leader if I myself had never actually done the same kind of thing? I loved that organization, and I love this book, so I took a deep breath and jumped.

I ended up being a copresident of SCBWI Western Washington for three successful years. Someone I barely knew stepped up to be copresident with me, and we became great friends. My team members from that experience are like family to me. I learned skills I never thought I could, gained a tremendous amount of self-confidence, experienced unbelievable personal growth, and had a ridiculous amount of fun doing it. Taking that role was one of the most positive, transformative decisions I have ever made, and I don't have a single regret.

If I can do it, so can you.

LET'S GO!

You've seen how Craig and Divine started something amazing while they were young. In addition to sharing more stories like theirs, this book will show you how you can do it, too. You'll learn how to choose a cause, recruit helpers, make a plan, manage your money, sell your ideas, and more! As Divine Bradley told New York's *Daily News*, "I didn't know exactly how to go about doing it. I just did it." And so can you.

It won't be easy, of course, but no matter what happens, some piece of your world will be better simply because you tried. You will make a difference to yourself and others. You'll gain new skills. You'll inspire people around you. You'll make new friends. And you'll have fun doing something you love while you solve a problem you care about.

Change is the process by which the future invades our lives.

Alvin Toffler, author, in his book *Future Shock*

3

The Secret Formula

You have to find something that you love enough to be able to take risks ... jump over the hurdles ... and break through the brick walls that are always going to be placed in front of you. If you don't have that ... you'll stop at the first giant hurdle.

George Lucas, movie producer, director, and writer, in an interview with the American Academy of Achievement in Washington DC on June 19, 1999

Changing anything—let alone the world—is a pretty tall order for anyone. Wouldn't it be nice if there was a secret formula for success? Sadly, there isn't. But there is a secret formula that will give you a better chance of being successful. It all comes down to your first decision ... and making sure it's a good one. That key piece of the puzzle is choosing what to do. Whether you come up with something that has never been tried before or put your own special twist on a tried-and-true classic, this chapter will help you find the perfect starting point.

ACTORES DE LA PREVENCIÓN
(PREVENTION ACTORS)

Florencia Manino, Facundo Pennesi, Marina Sananes, and Diana Calderón were studying theater at Argentina's National University of Cuyo when they got the idea for their venture. "We saw that there were a lot of car accidents due to excessive alcohol consumption in young people," they say. And they thought they could address the problem through theater. "We believe it is a real instrument of social development," they say, "because it makes people work together to achieve a common aim."

They contacted a local organization called Cable a Tierra (Ground Wire), an addiction prevention and rehabilitation center that provided the team with specific information about the problems related to alcohol and addiction. Then, after presenting their idea to Ashoka, an organization that invests in changemakers, they received the funding to start working.

Their group, Actores de la Prevención, created theater workshops that presented the risks associated with alcohol consumption. "The most fun and interesting thing was to manage how to get to young people deeply . . . trying to get to them by their interests," say the founders. Being in the play, acting the parts of characters in a club, made the participants feel like they were inside the problem.

Since the founders were already studying both theater and education, the hardest part of launching the venture was getting in touch with their audience. "The most difficult part was the distribution of the project and finding a way to reach schools who wanted the project," they say. "The bureaucracy of schools was difficult to deal with."

But they persisted. "What kept us going," they say, "was the idea of making a change in teenagers, the horror that is produced by this terrible problem, and the deaths in car accidents caused by the excess drinking of alcohol."

And they've now added a secondary goal: to empower future changemakers by teaching their students to question any social problems they encounter, identify their causes and consequences, and take an active role in solving them. "Our goal for the project is to get to the most places possible in order to make the message reach the biggest number of people," they say, "to plant the seeds of critical thought and self-knowledge in teenagers."

WHY THIS CHAPTER MATTERS

If you know you want to make a difference but just don't know where to begin, spend some time working through the exercises in this chapter. They'll help you get to know the most important player in your venture—you—so you can get some ideas and start putting together a solid plan. Thinking about your passions and skills will help you come up with the best idea to pursue.

On the other hand, maybe you picked up this book because you already have a problem you want to solve and are ready to get started. I still encourage you to read this chapter first to help you get in touch with your reasons for wanting to go that route and to clarify your approach. Doing these exercises before you jump in will make sure you've considered all the angles and get started down the best path.

WHAT'S YOUR PASSION?

Skin Care and Personal Care

As human beings, we like to think we are ruled by knowledge and logic. They certainly do have an effect on our choices and behavior, but there's something even deeper that truly controls us—emotion. Think about how many times you've done something you knew you probably shouldn't do, simply because it made you feel good. On the other hand, making yourself do something you don't enjoy can only last for so long, even if you know it's good for you.

What does this have to do with changing the world? Well, changing the world, even a small piece of it, is a pretty big undertaking. The only way for you to maintain enough energy and willpower to even attempt it is to tap into your most basic passions. "Try to do things and work with topics according to your interests, capacities, and abilities," says the Actores team. "When we do things with passion, we do things better." That is why Actores de la Prevención succeeded. The founders could have decided that their dream was too difficult to achieve, but instead they let their passion carry them forward to success.

Passion is what fuels power. If you feel passionately about something, you can't *not* do it. "The fact that we were studying acting helped us to prepare the theater play and allowed us to express an idea, using art to deeply touch the students," say the Actores team members. But they were also studying to be acting teachers, which was an important element. If they'd tried to just perform for the students, instead of enlisting the students themselves as actors, they might not have had the same success or taken their idea as far, because their project would have lacked the element of teaching that they also enjoyed.

To empower yourself, and others like you, it helps to find your passion first. So, how do you find that idea that is so *you* that you will not—cannot—quit, no matter what? Start by asking yourself some questions. What would you do if you could do anything you wanted? What do you love to do more than anything else? With these ideas in mind, you're ready to start brainstorming your passions.

Make Beauty Products

1. Start a venture journal, either in a bound book, a binder, or a computer document.

2. Make a list of all the things you enjoy doing like shopping, playing sports, playing video games, whatever—everything that gets you

20

excited or makes you happy. Be honest, even if it seems silly! If you don't start with something that really pumps you up, you'll run out of energy long before you cross the finish line.

3. Now let's expand that list even more. Look back at the list of things you love to do and ask yourself, "Why do I love doing that? What makes it fun for me?" Draw a line down the page just to the right of the first list. Write your answers to the right of that line. Keep asking yourself why, adding more columns, and filling them in until you can get to the fundamental reasons behind each of your passions. Do you love something because of the sense of danger, or maybe it's the feeling of security? Because you like solving complex puzzles, or perhaps because you like structure and predictability? Because you get to be alone, or rather because you enjoy being with other people?

All of this will help you find the perfect activity to keep you engaged and having fun.

WHAT ARE YOU GOOD AT?

Of course, you need more than passion to carry something through: you need skills! Actores wouldn't exist if the founders didn't know the first thing about theater, right? So let's make another list.

1. Go to a new page in your journal, and this time write down all the things you're good at. These can be from any area of your life: school, work, friends and family, sports and hobbies, everything you do! Is it easy for you to meet new people? Are you good at playing the piano or shooting hoops? Maybe you have a knack for designing websites. Do you always keep your room tidy and hand your homework in on time? Can you cook a healthy dinner for your family? Write down everything that crosses your mind, no matter how useless or commonplace it might seem to you.

2. Be sure to consider skills that involve people (babysitting, networking, or giving presentations), skills that involve things (playing basketball, scrapbooking, or caring for animals), and skills that involve information (working with spreadsheets, writing, or making videos). Also, think about physical skills (running, horseback riding, or dancing), mental skills (memorization, math, or songwriting), and interpersonal skills (mingling, interviewing, small talk, or giving speeches).

This list of skills will help you identify your strengths as you move forward.

WHAT NEEDS TO BE DONE?

Finally, let's identify a problem to solve.

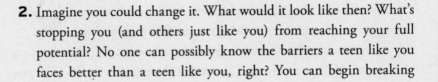

1. On the next page in your venture journal, write about problems you might be able to solve. Start by looking at yourself and your own life. What do you need? What do you and your friends complain about? What would you like to change?

2. Imagine you could change it. What would it look like then? What's stopping you (and others just like you) from reaching your full potential? No one can possibly know the barriers a teen like you faces better than a teen like you, right? You can begin breaking down those barriers now, for you and for those who will follow, like Actores did.

3. Now expand your focus a little bit and think about what's happening where you live. Consider your apartment building, street, block, or neighborhood. Do any problems come to mind? If you were in charge, what would you change first? What do you wish was available in your community that isn't there now? What other groups or resources aren't reaching their full potential? What do people need?

4. Keep widening your geographic scope—city, county, state, region, continent, whole world—and adding to your list of problems to solve until you've identified some issues that really get your emotions flowing. They might be emotions that feel negative, like anger or sadness, or they might be more positive emotions, like hope or pride. Are you outraged about a situation or an event, like Craig was about child labor? Are you afraid something bad might happen to you or one of your friends, like Divine was? Is there something you love doing, like the Actores do?

5. Put a star next to those issues that make you feel something intensely.

6. Now make a list of the other communities you belong to. *Community* can mean a lot of things. Usually, it means the geographic place where you live, but it might also be where you go to school, even if your school isn't in the same neighborhood as your home. It may be the school itself, and all the people in it. It might be a grade or class within that school, or a group or club (within the school or outside of it). Maybe it's the congregation of your church, or just the youth group there. Community can also be a wider group of people that you have something in common with, such as the LGBTQI community, *Doctor Who* enthusiasts, or high schoolers affected by cancer.

7. Next to each community you listed, write down one or more problems faced by that community. What do you really, truly wish you could fix for those communities? Maybe you've been in the foster care system and you have ideas about how it could work better. Perhaps your parents are from another country and you know how to help people still living there or other immigrants who came from there. Are your grandparents always asking you to teach them how to use the latest technology? Maybe other seniors could use the same kind of instruction.

No matter what form your venture takes, success will depend on identifying a need and solving a problem.

SOME AREAS TO THINK ABOUT

If you need a little help coming up with a list of problems, consider these broad categories to help you think about specific issues you might want to address:

- Animals
- Arts/culture
- Beauty — unattainable standards
- Bullying
- Children
- Civil rights
- Community
- Disabilities
- Domestic violence
- Drugs and alcohol
- Education — lack of
- Environment

- Fashion — *lack of representation*
- Health
- Homelessness ⟵ *self sustainability / job opportunities*
- Human rights *self care*
- Hunger
- Immigration
- Mental health
- Peace/war
- Racism — *job opportunities*
- Religion
- Safety
- Senior citizens
- Sexual abuse
- Sexual orientation
- Sports/athletics
- Technology
- Teen issues ⟵ *embarrassment / peer pressure*
- Transportation *acne*
- Violence
- Water purity — *indifference*
- Women's rights — *equal pay*

In My Experience

I've always loved words. When I was a kid, my favorite game was Scrabble. I delighted in hearing or reading new words and memorizing their meanings. I remember laughing when I first learned the word humongous. *I was pretty young, and* humongous *was one of the biggest words I'd ever heard. A huge word that means, well, "huge"— now that was funny!*

I've also always wanted to do *something. I remember lying awake at night wishing, praying, to find my talent—that one special thing that would allow me to make my mark on the world, to leave it better than I'd found it, to make a difference. I was good at a lot of things, but none of them jumped out as being particularly significant, and everyone told me that altruism and a love of words wouldn't earn me a living. So, lacking any obvious path, I instead followed the money.*

I became a software engineer. The pay was good. I had job security. I didn't even mind the work. But something was missing. I didn't really feel like I was making the world a better place. (Note: I rely on computers and software to do my job, and they're a big help to anyone trying to change the world these days, so I'm not saying they don't have a positive impact! I'm just saying I didn't personally feel that connection in my day-to-day work.) When my husband and I sold our first business and moved across the country, we decided to start a family while I took some time off to figure out what I wanted to do next.

While I was pregnant, I read everything I could get my hands on about parenting and babies. I felt so unprepared! I talked about what I learned with my friends who had children, and one day one of them said, "You should write this stuff down for people. You're good at finding all the facts and explaining them in a way that makes sense." It was like a lightbulb came on. I could do what I loved, use my skills, and give people something they wanted—all at the same time. I'd finally discovered my calling! I started to write.

I practiced for a long time before people started paying me to write, but it has been worth it. I've loved every minute of writing this book, and I hope it fills a need by helping you find your world-changing passion.

PASSION + SKILL + PROBLEM = VENTURE!

Now here's where it really gets fun! Let's consider how many ways the passions from your first list could intersect with the skills from your second list to address the problems on your third list. Here's where you get the energy, plus the ability, plus the motivation to make a difference.

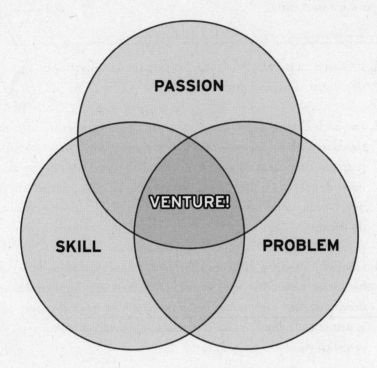

Here are some examples:

- Do you love to golf, know how to play it well, and want to help underprivileged kids? Launch a mentoring program that combines life skills and character education with golf instruction.

- Love hip-hop, know how to DJ, and want to address racism? Use music to unite people by putting on a dance that brings a message of diversity to your community.

- Enjoy knitting, know how to make scarves and hats, and worry about the plight of homeless people? Donate your handmade knitted items to a local homeless shelter.

Now it's your turn.

1. Pick an item from each of your lists to make a combination of passion, skill, and problem.

2. For each combination, come up with a specific venture idea that touches on all three words or phrases. Write it down in your venture journal. Your ideas might seem silly at first because they've never been done before. But don't worry. Maybe, just maybe, they've never been done before because *you* are the only one who can do them.

3. Continue choosing different items from each list, making new combinations, generating new venture ideas, and writing them in your notebook. You can choose items randomly or work through them systematically, but the idea is to make as many combinations as you can with the items on your lists.

That's all there is to it: start with something you love doing, add something you're already good at, and mix them with something you care a lot about. Tapping into the core of who you are will help you succeed and make sure you have a great time doing it. It won't feel like a chore. It will feel like a gift—something you feel both compelled and privileged to do.

ON YOUR WAY

By now you should have some pretty good ideas about how you might leave your own unique mark on your world . . . and have fun doing it. If you don't, spend some more time thinking about the exercises in this chapter and building your lists. You might want to sleep on it for a couple of days or talk it over with people who know you well. You can come back to this chapter and your lists whenever you need to until you feel like you've found a good fit.

When you've finally narrowed down your ideas to a few favorite combinations, it's time to turn the page! We'll analyze your options even more to help you decide which combination is the best one for you to work with.

The only time to grab hold of your dreams in this life is right now.

Liz Murray, *New York Times* bestselling author, inspirational speaker, and founder of Manifest Living, at We Day Seattle on March 27, 2013, attended by the author

| 4 |
Researching Your Big Ideas

I will not follow where the path may lead, but I will go where there is no path, and I will leave a trail.

Muriel Strode, poet, in "Wind-Wafted Flowers,"
first printed in *The Open Court*, volume 17, no. 8 in 1903

So far, you've identified some problems you might want to focus on and how your passions and skills can support each cause. Hopefully, you're all fired up and ready to get started! Before you go any farther, though, take some time to stop and get your bearings. Trust me—you'll be glad you did. A little research now can help you pick just the right project to focus on, and some preparation up front can save you tons of time and effort down the road. And, who knows? You might just discover an important detour, like Rhiannon and Madison did with Project ORANGS . . .

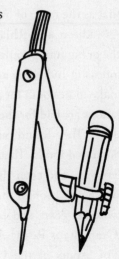

PROJECT ORANGS

Friends Rhiannon Tomtishen and Madison Vorva, from Ann Arbor, Michigan, decided to work together to earn their Girl Scout Bronze Award. To earn that, girls must identify a problem, build a team, plan a solution, take action, and share their experience with their community. They'd both been inspired by Dr. Jane Goodall's work with chimpanzees, so Rhiannon and Madison started out by going to RootsandShoots.org, Dr. Goodall's website for young people, to learn about what other kids around the country were doing for the environment, people, and animals. From there, they surfed the internet to research other types of endangered animals, especially other great apes.

"Both of us sat there with tears in our eyes as we read stories and looked at photos of orangutans that had been killed or attacked as a result of the palm oil industry," they say. "Our outrage led us to choose that as the topic of our Bronze Award."

Madison and Rhiannon discovered that one of the main threats to the orangutan population is the destruction of their native habitat, rainforests in Indonesia and Malaysia. These rainforests are being cleared to make more room for palm oil plantations. They learned that these plantations are bad for the animals, the environment, and the people around them. They found out that palm oil is a common ingredient in many processed foods. They started checking labels on products they encountered . . . and then they noticed palm oil on the ingredients list of the Girl Scout cookies they had been selling since they were little! The girls switched gears and launched a new venture called Project ORANGS (Orangutans Really Appreciate and Need Girl Scouts) to convince the Girl Scouts of the United States to switch to deforestation-free and socially responsible sources of palm oil.

Since then, they've learned even more. "The palm oil industry is very complex and there are many sides of the story, so it has been difficult to know exactly what information to trust," they say. "We have done our best to talk to as many involved parties as possible and assemble a team of experts from organizations that we trust. For example, when we first started raising awareness about the orangutan we reached out to Orangutan Outreach, a related organization, and have worked with them since. We've also worked closely with the Union of Concerned Scientists and the Climate Advisers to familiarize ourselves with the policy and scientific sides of the palm oil industry."

Despite all the serious research they've done on the topic, Rhiannon and Madison have been dismissed and criticized. One writer even called them "little do-gooders" and said decisions like these are "best left up to adults." Plus, the girls have had to learn how to balance the time spent on Project ORANGS with their schoolwork and social lives. They'll be the first to admit that it hasn't always been easy. "It has been our passion for this cause," they say, "that has allowed us to persevere through the tough moments."

Besides gaining courage, confidence, and leadership skills, Rhiannon and Madison know they have made a real difference. In 2011 the Girl Scouts of the United States adopted a sustainable palm oil policy, and Project ORANGS continues to raise awareness for its cause and educate consumers about the issues regarding palm oil. When Rhiannon and Madison first started, they used a homemade poster board and gave presentations in their siblings' classrooms. Now Project ORANGS has grown into a national platform, and that may be only the beginning of what these two accomplish.

Madison says, "The past seven years have taught me necessary leadership skills that I will apply to my future career and aspirations." And Rhiannon agrees, saying, "Although I may not work on the palm oil issue my entire life, I know that the skills and lessons I've learned will always stay with me."

GETTING STARTED

Like Rhiannon and Madison, odds are you will need to find out a bit more about the problems you've identified or the groups you hope to serve before you can decide which of your big ideas to pursue. You should understand the history behind each issue and be able to identify all of the major players, and that requires research. Let's take a closer look at your big ideas and try to identify what you still need to investigate.

1. For each of the remaining ideas on your narrowed-down list of passion, skill, and problem combinations, answer the following questions in your venture journal:

- Who might support your cause and why?

- Who might *oppose* your cause and why?

- Who is making the decisions now?

- Why are they making those choices?

- Who are they affecting, and what do those affected *really* need?

- What's the best way to help them?

- Do they know they need help?

- Do they even want help?

2. What resources are already available to those affected by this problem, and to you as you try to solve it?

Some of these questions might seem trivial at first, or even just plain stupid. I mean, who could possibly be opposed to ending child labor, right? Ah, but of course, there are the (sometimes very powerful and never very nice!) people who chain children like Iqbal to carpet mills in the first place. Whatever, or whomever, you're fighting for or against, you're going to want to make sure you have a good view of the big picture before you start. This foundation will help guide all of your decisions along the way.

Now, keep writing! Journal about everything you already know, and then make special notes about any questions you think you'll need to answer. As you answer those questions and learn more about your issues, you'll probably find new questions to ask. Make sure to write the new questions—and their answers—in your journal as you come to them so nothing gets lost.

SAVE EVERYTHING!

As you research, keep in mind that all of this information isn't just for you, and it isn't just for right now. Everything you learn at this stage will come in handy later whenever you need to educate others about your venture or prove that you know what you're talking about. So research well now, and be sure to organize and store all the information as you go so you can find it next time you need it. Whether your venture journal is on the computer or in a binder full of papers, organization is key.

INTERNET

Luckily, your generation has more access than ever to powerful tools that can help you find information. One of the easiest ways to start your research is, of course, on the internet. Use a search engine such as Google or Bing to find sites related to your causes. Wikipedia can also be a great place to start looking for background information, but be aware that there aren't necessarily experts checking everything that's written on Wikipedia. Be sure to look at the sources listed at the bottom of the page and follow those links to get to the original information. Finally, if there are already established organizations related to your issues, such as UNICEF or the World Wildlife Fund, they can be a big help, too.

As I'm sure you know, websites from universities (.edu), government (.gov), and nonprofits (.org) are usually the most trustworthy, but always question why any given site is providing the information it does. You might question an industry group when it comes to presenting the latest research related to its industry. For example, the National Pork Board says, "According to a new study published in the February journal *Obesity*, Purdue University researchers found that including protein from lean pork in your diet can help you lose weight." Your conclusion might be that the benefit came from eating pork instead of other meats, but look again. Is that what it really says? Notice that the National Pork Board doesn't quote the original article. If you want to know the whole truth, you'd better go read the article that it's referring to, so you know what the researchers actually reported. In this case, you'd find that the study, which was funded by the National Pork Board, actually concluded that the test group that ate a higher percentage of pork protein lost the same amount of weight as the group that ate a higher percentage of carbo-hydrates, but the pork group lost less lean body mass and reported feeling more full. See the difference? It didn't test against other kinds of meat, and the pork group didn't lose any more weight. The same goes for non-profit organizations. The groups posting the statistic may be motivated to pick and choose from only those studies that paint them in the best light. Always make sure you find original, trustworthy sources for the data.

Beyond those general starting points, you might also find groups on sites like Google Groups or Yahoo where people are actively discussing your issues. You can also search social networking sites like Tumblr, Twitter, and Facebook, and then get involved in online discussions about your issues or interests. This can often lead you directly to the key players, and give you unprecedented access to them. With social media, it's usually best to follow other people's discussions for a while before jumping in. Try to get involved gradually by introducing yourself and commenting here and there. Eventually you'll feel like you know enough to ask good questions, and people will know you well enough to want to help. Just remember your manners and treat online environments the same as you would their real-world counterparts. After all, you wouldn't crash a party where everyone else knew each other, jump up on the table, and start yelling out questions, would you?

You may have heard the saying, "On the internet, no one knows you're a dog." Well, no one knows you're a young person, either. Sometimes, this can work to your advantage, as people will often take you more seriously if they think you're an adult. Don't misrepresent yourself, of course, and never tell an outright lie. This goes both ways, of course. Don't assume that the people you're talking to are really who they say they are. Stay safe! NEVER give out any personal information over the internet or agree to meet anyone by yourself.

As you find relevant materials online, remember to save them for later. There are many services out there to help you do just that. One of my favorites is Evernote, but there are plenty of other options such as Delicious and Diigo. And, of course, you can always just store book-marks in your browser if you're surfing on your own computer, or print information out on paper and store it in files like we used to do in the old days.

CONDUCTING INTERVIEWS

One of the most important sources of information is personal inter-views. Don't be afraid to go out and talk to the experts on your topics, including those who have the problems and those who may have the power to change things. If you want to address hunger in your community, for example, call your local food bank and ask about its most pressing needs. Or, if you want to work to protect an endangered species, like Rhiannon and Madison did, you might contact a zookeeper, the head of an existing animal welfare agency, or a knowledgeable university professor.

Interviewing experts doesn't need to be as intimidating as it might sound. Believe it or not, most people enjoy talking about themselves and are honored to share their stories with others. You just need to find them. To do that, you can use internet searches, web pages, and librarians to help you track down the right people and their contact information. You can make phone calls, send emails, write letters, or schedule in-person meetings (but only agree to meet in person if you can do so safely—in a public place and with an adult or buddy!). No matter which approach you take, make sure you:

- Research first! How many of the questions from the first section in this chapter can you answer yourself? Don't waste other people's time by asking them questions that you can easily find answers to elsewhere. Save the experts for the really hard questions that only they can answer. Respect their time and they'll respect you—plus you'll learn about new, deeper questions that you may not have thought to ask otherwise.

- Prepare a list of questions you want to ask, based on your original questions list and the research you've already done. This will help you stay on track and not forget anything important. Some of the questions related to a problem or issue could be hard for your interview subject to talk about. Try to put yourself in his or her shoes. Don't avoid questions because they may be sensitive topics, but be thoughtful and compassionate when you ask them.

- Write yourself a script and practice ahead of time so you are confident and ready to make a good impression.

- Introduce yourself and highlight your connection (if any) to the person you're interviewing. For example, you might start with, "Hi, my name is Trevor. My uncle suggested I contact you because of your past experience working with the circus."

- State your purpose and ask your questions. Tell the interviewee you're researching a topic (in the above example, perhaps it's about the treatment of circus elephants) and you want to talk to an expert to find out the real story (are the elephants really abused?).

- Listen! In between questions, don't feel like you have to talk to fill in the silence. It's okay to allow other people time to think and compose their answers, even if it feels a little awkward or uncomfortable to you. Often the people you're interviewing will jump in to fill any pauses, giving you more information than they would have otherwise.

- Let the conversation flow naturally, even if it feels like you're veering away from the prepared questions. For one thing, it's useful to establish a friendly rapport when you're interviewing. Also, these unplanned exchanges are often more genuine and straight from the heart than the preplanned questions and answers, so they can be the most valuable part of the interview. When you feel like the unplanned detour has run its course, just refer to your list of questions to get back on track.

- Conclude with an open-ended question, such as, "Can you think of anything important that I might be missing?" Or, "Is there anyone else I should talk to about this issue?"

- Proofread all emails and printed letters carefully before you send them!

- Record all of the details, including the date, the location, the person's contact information (especially the correct spelling of his or her name!), and the answers to your questions. You can take quick handwritten notes on paper, type on a laptop, or record the conversation to listen to later. Recording is the best option, because you won't be distracted with note taking and can focus on the conversation. Always ask permission before recording someone, though! Whichever method you choose, store the results of the interview in a safe place such as an online storage solution or in your venture journal.

- Thank the person for sharing his or her time and expertise with you.

In My Experience

When I became a professional writer, my first assignments were articles for magazines. These articles relied on interviewing experts, synthesizing the information, and structuring it into a readable report. Most people don't know it, but I'm extremely shy and introverted, so that first step—interviewing experts—was a doozy for me! How could little old me just call up experts and get them to talk to me? But I had to give it a try in order to get my new career off the ground.

What I discovered has affected every interaction I have with someone new. People love being asked about what they do and what they care about! They appreciate the fact that someone is taking an interest in them. It validates their efforts and tells them that what they're doing is important. Remember, it's not about you. You're asking people for their opinions, and more often than not, they'll be happy to tell you— just because you asked.

SURVEYS

Another useful way to collect opinions from the people involved with your issues is to conduct a survey. If you'll see people in person, you can make your survey in any word processing program and just print out enough copies for them each to have one. Be sure to let them know how they can return the completed survey to you, whether in person, in an anonymous box, or by mail. Or, if your target audience is online, you can design your survey on a website like SurveyMonkey.com and send it by email. In either case, here are some things to remember when designing your survey:

- Give it a descriptive title so people will know what the survey is about at a glance.

- If you have room, include a short description of who you are, why you're doing the survey, and how you will use the results.

- State up front whether the results will be anonymous or not.

- Keep it as short and simple as possible! If it looks too complicated or time-consuming, people won't do it.

- Try to ask mostly specific, detailed questions with yes/no or multiple-choice answers.

- But be sure to leave at least one open-ended question, such as: Is there anything else you would like to add?

- Always thank participants for their input!

You might want to design a few different surveys for various groups involved with your issues. For example, if you think there aren't enough after-school activities at your school, you could survey the students to see what types of activities they would be interested in and survey the teachers to see what types of activities they could offer. Or, if you're going to tackle the issue of hunger in your community, you might survey local businesses to see if they'd be interested in donating leftover food, and you could survey area food banks to see what types of food they need most.

Compile the results of your survey in an easy-to-read report, and file the report in your online storage solution or in your venture journal.

OTHER RESEARCH OPTIONS

The library is another helpful resource. Most libraries have access to databases with articles from professional journals, magazines, and newspapers so you can read the latest research about your topics. Your library may have subscriptions to academic journals, which are peer reviewed—checked over by other people in the same field of study—so you'll know they're trustworthy. Look for related magazines and newspaper articles. You can also, of course, look for books on the topics. Just be sure to check the copyright dates to make sure the information is current. Don't be afraid to ask a librarian to help you! That is what they are there for, after all. They can help you find resources, sometimes even from other libraries, and they may be plugged in to other resources in the community as well. Reference librarians specialize in questions like these, but any librarian ought to be able to help you use the library to answer specific research questions.

This type of research will be more applicable to some subjects than others. For example, if your idea is to throw birthday parties for low-income children, you probably wouldn't need to do much library research. On the other hand, you would need to thoroughly research anything dealing with science—such as a health or environmental issue—at a library to make sure you have all the most accurate, up-to-date information.

You may also find useful information about problems in your community in archived articles from your local newspaper. Look for how other communities addressed problems similar to yours and for surveys related to your ideas that were conducted by other people or organizations. If you're not even sure where to start researching the issues, explain your ideas to the reference librarian and ask if she has any suggestions.

As with your other research, save everything either online or in your journal so you can access it later.

THERE CAN BE ONLY ONE . . . FOR NOW

Research your ideas from chapter 3 in this way until you've answered all the questions you can and have a good understanding of each of them. Now, let's try to narrow your ideas down to just one project to work on.

1. Do any of the project ideas feel too big or overwhelming? Look through your research notes to see if there's a way to focus on just a portion of the problem and tackle that piece first. For example, if you want to address childhood cancer, you might initially focus on helping children who are in the hospital receiving cancer treatment. This might lead to new, more manageable, project ideas.

2. Now, look through your research notes for each project idea again. Do any of the ideas still have too many unanswered questions? If so, you can cross them off the list. You probably won't be able to solve a problem if you don't have enough information to fully understand it.

3. For each of the remaining project ideas, ask yourself questions like:

- Which one sounds the most fun, interesting, or rewarding?

- Which one could make the biggest difference or benefit the most people?

- Which one has the best chance of succeeding? (Note: Don't worry too much about success or failure right now! I only mention this because if you have competing ideas, it might be a useful tie-breaker.)

Now you just need to choose one! If you're feeling particularly torn between two or more ideas, pretend for a minute that you chose one of them. How does that choice make you feel? Do that for each option, and then go with the one you felt the best about. And don't worry—you can always go back and try a different idea sometime in the future!

Once you have one idea that you've thoroughly researched and are ready to commit to, move on to chapter 5 and let's start building your team.

The first thing you have to do if you want to change the world is understand it.

Martin Sheen, actor and activist, in a press conference at
We Day Seattle on March 27, 2013, attended by the author

| 5 |

Building Your Dream Team

People are the most important part of any organization . . . . At the end of the day, leadership is getting people to use their full talents to support your shared objective.

Colin Powell, former US Secretary of State,

in *State Magazine*, February 2002

Launching a venture is a big undertaking, and you may have noticed that the first thing many venturers do is enlist the help of others. Craig made a presentation to his class and asked for volunteers, Divine worked with his friends, and Rhiannon and Madison knew they wanted to work together from the beginning.

Change always starts with just one person: in this case, you! But only when people join together for a cause can change really take root, spread across a community or society, and stand the test of time. Plus, it'll be a whole lot easier—and more fun—if you recruit some friends or other like-minded peers to help you out! You'll want people who can help you bounce ideas around and brainstorm plans. You'll need people who have skills and strengths that you don't. And, of course, more people doing the work means more work will actually get done!

RICHARD'S RWANDA

When Jessica Markowitz was just eleven years old, Richard Kananga, a human rights activist from Rwanda, came to stay with her family in Seattle, Washington. Richard told Jessica about the war in his country and how it had left many of the children there—especially girls—orphaned, poor, and at risk of becoming victims of crime and disease. Jessica couldn't stop thinking about what it would be like to live there. *Somebody should do something!* she thought. As it turned out, that somebody was her.

Jessica researched the situation in Rwanda, made a slideshow to present what she had learned, and shared it with her sixth-grade class. Her friends and peers agreed with her: something had to be done, even if they had to do it themselves! When they learned that girls in Rwanda were often prevented from going to school, they founded the all-girl group Richard's Rwanda to help girls in the rural village of Nyamata, where Richard's cousin was a teacher. Richard's Rwanda hoped that those girls would one day become leaders in their impoverished community and contribute both financially and socially.

The group applied for grants, hosted bake sales, and organized other fundraising events, and eventually took money to Rwanda to pay for the girls' school fees. Richard's Rwanda was working hard, meeting goals, and gaining recognition. The venture was a clear success. Then, after three years of working together all throughout middle school, Jessica and her friends graduated. The close, dedicated team found itself split across five different area high schools.

That might have been the end for Richard's Rwanda, but instead, the founders turned it into an opportunity for growth. They recruited new members and eventually launched a new chapter of Richard's Rwanda at each of their five high schools.

Today, the organization Jessica started in 2007 with a simple presentation to her class has grown to include about one hundred teens—girls and boys—from different middle and high schools across the country, and it is still growing. Richard's Rwanda formed a partnership with a mentor school in the city of Kigali, Rwanda, which now has its own Richard's Rwanda chapter and helps support the girls in Nyamata. They hold fundraising events, organize community outreach and awareness projects, and send high school students on a service learning trip to Rwanda every summer. To date, they've raised more than $130,000.

Now Richard's Rwanda is an official 501(c)(3) charitable organization. Jessica is grateful to have the support of an experienced board of directors to help guide the group through upcoming challenges, such as sustaining the integrity and value of the organization as she and the other founders graduate from high school and move on to college. Continuing to recruit in middle schools and bringing new leadership up through the ranks will contribute to the organization's potential for impact as well as its ongoing stability.

But it all started with Jessica. Her advice to other young people who want to do something like this? As she told Deborah Reber on HeartofGoldGirls.com, "Always remember that when it seems like you're in a situation where there's nothing you as an individual can do, don't doubt yourself—you have no idea where your personal inspiration will go . . . I think it's important to hold your head up and be proud of what you're doing because in the end you're the one who's changing people's lives."

COMMON POSITIONS AND TITLES

As you build your team, allow people to specialize and have ownership of their positions. You can define any roles you want, and some of your needs will depend on your particular goals, but there are a few common positions to have in mind from the start. These include founder, secretary, treasurer, technical support, public relations, and volunteer coordinator. Here's a description of each of these titles:

- Founder: This is you! The leader of the venture sets the tone for the organization, offers support and encouragement to the team, and is ultimately responsible for the group's activities.

- Secretary: The team's secretary is responsible for keeping track of what happens at every meeting and then sending his notes, called minutes, out to the entire team. He should also organize copies of the minutes from all of the team's meetings in a central location. This helps you and your team remember what you've accomplished as well as learn from your past mistakes and successes. It helps missing team members keep up with what's happening and gets new members up to speed more quickly, too. Can't remember why you decided to sell candy bars instead of cookies? Go back to those meeting minutes for a reminder. The secretary should be able to write or type quickly and be a good listener.

- Treasurer: Simply put, the treasurer is responsible for keeping track of the money. This means she has access to the bank account and is comfortable with budgets. The treasurer needs to be very organized, responsible, and—obviously—someone you would trust with your wallet.

- Technical Support: Just about everything we do these days relies on technology in one way or another, so it's a big plus if you have someone on your team who is curious about, and willing to play with, technology. The technical guru might be the one who explores new project management tools, sets up spreadsheets, creates your team's social media accounts, designs slideshows, builds your website, and so on. He doesn't need to have all of these skills ready to go from day one, of course, but it will be invaluable to have someone who can help you figure these kinds of things out as you need them.

- Public Relations: This person is responsible for advertising and marketing your venture. This might involve designing flyers; making posters; sending press releases; putting together presentations; giving speeches; or contributing to social media networks, the website, and the blog. There will probably be a fair amount of overlap with your technical guru—a lot of times the public relations person comes up with the marketing ideas, and the technical guru makes them a reality—so make sure both people can work well together. You might also consider dividing the public relations role among two or more team members. For example, maybe you have a talented artist who would be great with the flyers and posters but hates public speaking. If you pair him with the class clown who loves to be on stage, you'll have your public relations needs in the bag.

- Volunteer Coordinator: This team member is responsible for recruiting new team members and keeping existing team members engaged. She should be outgoing and comfortable interacting with people.

As you build your team, assign people to some of these key roles so they can specialize and not step on each other's toes. The positions will likely evolve as your team members get to know each other and you work together to set a mission statement, so think of these definitions as guidelines and be ready to redefine titles and job descriptions as necessary.

When you're assigning roles, consider people's skills and interests as well as their personalities. You don't want to ask the artistic type to set up spreadsheets, or make a shy person the public speaker. Think about who might be more of a take-charge leader and who might be more of a worker bee. You can use all different kinds of people, but assign the roles wisely so there aren't any fundamental conflicts.

WHAT TO LOOK FOR

You already know what you like to do and what skills you have, thanks to the lists you made in your venture journal in chapter 3. You'll put these to good use as you start, build, and maintain your venture. Nobody can be good at everything, though, and a successful team depends on members with a diverse set of skills. You need to find people who complement you, who have strengths in the areas where you are weaker. Let's go back to your journal again, but this time, think about what you *don't* like to do and what you're *not* very good at. You guessed it: it's time to make some more lists!

1. Reread your lists of passions and skills in your venture journal. If you think of anything you didn't include when you first made the lists, add it now.

2. Now look at the common roles previously defined and make a list of the ones you could do but wouldn't enjoy very much.

3. Finally, write down the roles that you know other people would be better at than you would be.

Don't be too hard on yourself, but try your best to be honest. Remember, no one expects you to love or be amazing at everything. And you'll be better off if you identify and recognize your dislikes and weaknesses up front so you can find the best people to help you. A soccer team isn't going to win many games with a team full of amazing goalies, nor can everyone on a football team be a quarterback. The key to building a successful team is finding people to fill all the necessary positions.

WHO TO ASK

Do you already know anyone who might be able to fill in some of the gaps in your skill set? Think about the people you interact with every day at school, in your activities, or at home.

You should also think about reaching out to people you may not know as well but who might feel passionate about the same issue as you. Consider your friends, classmates, sports teams, and members of your clubs or groups. Don't forget your local youth centers and even online circles, if you're already active there. Of course, you can also ask your family—especially brothers and sisters. Even adults like parents, teachers, coaches, and pastors can help you find team members, since they might know other young people who have interests similar to yours.

Consider diversity. The strongest teams include many different kinds of people from different backgrounds. That way, everyone brings something different to the table: a fresh perspective, a unique skill, diverse connections in the community. Be open and accepting when someone new expresses an interest in joining you. The key quality to look for when you're building your team is passion. If your team members aren't as committed to the cause as you are, they could weigh you down instead of helping you along. Remember, the best way to be great in anything is to surround yourself with great people!

Use your venture journal to take notes on all the people you think could help you build your team.

HOW TO ASK

Now that you have some ideas for who would be good additions to your team and how you can get in touch with them, it's time to decide how to invite them to join your venture. The first thing you need to do is obvious—ask! This might sound daunting, but remember all the reasons why you're interested in launching a venture in the first place. Anyone who joins your team will likely have similar reasons of their own—and get similar rewards. So, don't think of it as though you are bothering people or begging them for help. Instead, you are offering them a chance to be real-life superheroes! Opportunities like *that* don't come along every day. How lucky can they be?

All of that work you did in chapters 3 and 4 comes into play here, too. To connect with like-minded peers, be sure to use both your passion and the facts. People are much more likely to follow someone who tells a powerful story. You can do that by sweeping them away with your enthusiasm and then backing it up with your research to convince them that you are on the right track.

ELEVATOR PITCH

A good tool for telling people about your venture is known as an elevator pitch—a short summary that you could deliver to a stranger during the time it takes to ride an elevator, about thirty seconds. You'll give your elevator pitch over and over again—every time you meet someone new, from now when you're inviting people to join your venture, to years down the road when people ask how you got started with it.

1. To create your elevator pitch, focus on only the most important aspects of your venture. Take a few minutes to write the answers to these questions in your venture journal:

   • What is your venture called?

   • What are you trying to do, why, and for whom?

- What do you need right now?

2. Incorporate your answers into one or two complete sentences. Tell an engaging story that is relevant to your listener.

3. Condense your message until you can say it in thirty seconds or less. For example, Jessica might have said, "Richard's Rwanda hopes to educate and empower girls in Rwanda so they can help rebuild their country. We need someone to organize our next fundraiser so a group of girls from Washington, DC, can travel to Rwanda next summer."

4. Finally, practice the end result until you can say it in your sleep. You'll be glad you did the next time you ask someone to join your team or when someone you've just met asks you, "So, what do you do?" You'll have the perfect answer and will be able to deliver it flawlessly, hopefully gaining a new supporter in the process.

After you've said your elevator pitch about your venture and its goal, appeal to the skills of the person you want to join you, and call him to action. It's okay to let him know that you have a weakness or two. Don't be afraid to tell him how much your venture needs his particular skills and how valuable his contribution would be to the team. Let him know it won't be easy. Lay it out fully and honestly. There will be real work involved, and it will take time away from other things in his life. But it's all for a worthy cause. Remember: the harder the work, the bigger the reward.

HOLES IN THE ROLES

As you recruit team members, ask people which of the roles they are most interested in leading or assisting with before you make assignments.

Allow people to choose their own roles when possible. You might find it works best to have a lot of overlap and sharing of responsibilities, especially if you have a small team. A single team member could fill more than one role, or she could lead one role while assisting with another. Ideally, you'll fill every position with someone who will get the job done, while also allowing team members to contribute to the areas they're most interested in or skilled at.

After you have made the assignments, write a formal summary of what you think each person is responsible for and give all of the descriptions to every team member. This will ensure that everyone has a clear set of expectations, which will avoid surprises and misunderstandings later on.

DON'T WORRY IF YOU DON'T HAVE IT ALL

When you're done recruiting teammates and assigning position titles, there will most likely be some roles that aren't filled or some skills that the team lacks. That's perfectly okay. Start working with the people you have, and you'll find ways to patch up any remaining holes later. Can't find anyone who knows how to set up a website? No problem. Maybe your adult mentor (see chapter 6) will be able to help, or you can build it into your budget (chapter 8) to hire someone. Just make a note of what you're missing so you don't forget it later, and continue onward!

BEING A LEADER

At this point, you might feel a little overwhelmed. Maybe you have a great team lined up with all the roles filled by enthusiastic and capable volunteers, but you feel less than confident about being the "boss." Or, maybe you have some friends who are willing to pitch in, but you know you're going to be wearing several hats in order to get everything done, at least for now. Perhaps you're going it alone and you *know* that each and every one of those roles is going to be filled by one person—you. In any case, it's only natural to wonder what you're getting yourself into, and if you have what it takes to pull it off. I absolutely believe that you can do it. And this book will help you.

LEADERSHIP TIPS

So, how do you become a great leader? It's really not that hard. The key is to recognize that you're not there to boss people around. Instead, you're there to build a team with common goals and to help everyone succeed.

Several years later, my son still talks about his favorite teacher from elementary school. Her classroom was always under perfect control, her young students were calmly respectful to her and to each other, and they always strove to do their very best work. The casual observer might have assumed she was strict and overbearing. Yet it was clear her students adored her. My son says, "She's my favorite teacher ever, because she never told us what to do. She just inspired us to do it—so we did." That is true leadership.

To be a good leader, you just need to remember a few basic concepts:

- Listen: Make sure you let your team members express themselves. Ask a lot of questions. Listen carefully to the answers. Before you speak, give yourself time to think about how things might be interpreted, or misinterpreted.

- Include others: People want to feel useful and appreciated! Let them contribute in the best ways they can, and then make sure to acknowledge those contributions.

- Stay passionate: Remember why you chose this venture in the first place and what you hope to accomplish. If you maintain your own enthusiasm and let it show, your teammates will keep up theirs.

THE MAGIC WORDS

Remember, even though you're asking people to volunteer, basic manners go a long way. Be sure to say please and thank you every chance you get—both now, when you're asking people to join your cause, and after they've already put in hours of their time to help it along.

Praise people for their time and effort. Recognize their contributions. Reward them in whatever meaningful ways you can. Note that this doesn't have to be money or anything expensive. It could be a handwritten note or handmade card from you, or a shout-out on a social media site, or maybe help with something they need done. People like to feel appreciated, and these small efforts on your part can have huge payoffs in terms of team engagement and loyalty.

In My Experience

I recently saw Paul McCartney in concert. One of the original members of the Beatles, he's been a rock 'n' roll icon since before you—or I—were born. How many shows has he performed? How many millions of screaming fans has he played for? Yet he was clearly surprised and humbled by the forty-five thousand people on their feet for him. Currently in his seventies, he worked harder than I've ever seen a musician work on stage to ensure he put on a good show and gave us our money's worth. It was obviously on his mind throughout the concert.

At one point he interrupted the performance to thank his fellow band members, as most front men do. But he didn't stop there. He thanked the lighting crew, the camera people, the sound technicians, the security guards keeping us all safe, the guy who handed him a different guitar when he needed one, the people who set up the stage and the speakers and the screens . . . His list went on and on until finally he thanked the truck drivers who haul all the people and all the stuff around the country just so he can do what he loves: play music for us. He choked up a bit on that last part, clearly beholden to all of the people whose efforts behind the scenes support him while he's in the spotlight.

Now I don't know, of course, but I'm guessing that most of those people—from the roadies to the band to the managers—would follow Sir Paul McCartney just about anywhere, simply because he noticed them, said thank you, and meant it.

WHAT IF THINGS DON'T WORK OUT?

One of the nice things about being the leader is that your venture is just that—yours! Don't worry about being stuck with these people forever. You may find out that one of your team members just isn't committed enough. Or perhaps you've always had fun hanging out with him, but you discover that you don't work well together. Or maybe she oversold her skills and really can't deliver what she promised.

Before you ask people like this to leave the team, though, think about ways you might help them be more successful. Maybe you haven't given them clear enough instructions. Would a different role, or a pared-down one with less responsibility, be a better fit? If they have the passion and energy, it's worth your while to try to find a way for them to put that to use. If you truly can't find a good way to accommodate them, then you'll have to ask them to leave the team. Make it clear that you value their contributions up to this point. Let them know—gently—why it's not working out. And if you still want to be friends, make sure you let them know that you'd still like to get together when you're not working on the venture! With a little praise, sensitivity, and tact, you can ease out of a sticky situation with no hard feelings on either side.

On the flip side, if people want off the team, it's best not to fight them even if they brought seemingly irreplaceable skills to the table. Remember that whole passion thing? If they don't feel enthusiastic, they're not going to give it their best effort, and that probably isn't going to work out in the long run. And you certainly don't need anyone's negative energy impacting your decisions or the cause you're trying to help. Whatever you do, don't take it personally. People have lots of different reasons for pulling back from a commitment, and it most likely has more to do with their personal interest level and outside time pressures than their actual support, or lack of it, for you or the venture. Likewise, there's no reason to hold a grudge or unfriend them. Just be grateful they had the courage to be honest. It's okay to express your disappointment, but then thank them for their efforts so far, wish them well—and mean every word.

Sticks in a bundle are unbreakable.

Kenyan proverb

| 6 |
Enlisting a Savvy Adult

**If I hadn't had mentors,
I wouldn't be here today. I'm a product of
great mentoring, great coaching . . .**

Indra Nooyi, CEO of PepsiCo, at the Catalyst Awards
Conference in New York City on April 9, 2008

Hopefully now you have a great team of young people in place to help you. You're almost ready to jump in! Before you do, there's at least one more person you need on your team—an adult. Like it or not, there are still some things only an adult can do—like sign contracts or other legal documents—so you must find at least one adult who is willing and able to help you out.

Profile
GREENING FORWARD

When Charles Orgbon was twelve years old, the students at his school in Florence, South Carolina, were required to complete a service project. Charles noticed his school had a problem with litter, so he started picking up trash by himself.

Soon, he recruited helpers and formed a club called Earth Savers. As the club became more successful, Charles decided it was time to share what he had learned online, so other young people could start environmental clubs in their own schools. He knew that having a great mentor is one of the biggest boosts for someone launching a new venture, so he wanted to start a website that could serve as a virtual mentor for other environmentally-minded young people like himself.

For a long time, it was just Charles working on the website all by himself. But then he made a connection that changed the shape of his venture. Charles's principal had a niece who was doing an internship with Earth Force, a national organization whose mission is "to engage young people as active citizens who improve the environment and their communities now and in the future." The intern suggested that Charles call Dr. Lisa Bardwell, the CEO of Earth Force. It was the only connection he had to any environmental leaders, so Charles decided he might as well give it a shot. To his surprise, it worked! Lisa started following him and his efforts, which led to Earth Force offering Charles a position on their board and many other opportunities.

Today, a CEO himself at age seventeen, Charles oversees a team of thirteen people, has a board of advisors, and is personally involved with many other environmental groups and activities. His Earth Savers clubs have enabled over 1,500 youth in more than a dozen communities in the United States, Africa, and Asia to recycle more than sixty tons of waste, plant more than two hundred trees, and save 155,000 gallons of water. Altogether, Earth Savers has involved over ten thousand people in its campaigns. GreeningForward.org, Charles's main website, has more than fifty partners, shares knowledge and research about environmental issues, connects young environmentalists from all around the world, and has trained thousands of youth on how to initiate their own local environmental projects.

Charles's advice for youth embarking on their own ventures? "You need a mentor," he says. "Be bold and brave and call!" Charles is grateful he decided to make that call. "I can't put a value on all the places I've been and people I've met," he says. "Greening Forward has given purpose to my life, and I know what I want to do with my life. It's a very exciting, exciting journey—and I have a lot of fun doing it!"

WHY YOU NEED AN ADULT MENTOR

Just like Charles, many successful entrepreneurs say the most useful thing they had when they were starting out was a good mentor. This is even more important for a young person, since a mentor will have experience that you don't. An adult can discuss the merits of your various ideas with you, give useful feedback, and help you avoid common mistakes.

FINDING A MENTOR

There are potential mentors all around you. "Mentors are a lot closer than you may think," Charles says. "A mentor can be anyone, even just someone you can talk to about things." Charles recommends thinking about who you are now and picturing who could help make you the best you can be. "Think about where you are looking for growth," he says, "and find people who have those skills." And, he adds, find out who *their* mentors were! Let's make a list of people you might want to ask for help.

1. Get your venture journal and make a new list of possible mentors.

2. Start by considering those closest to you: your parents or other family members. Do any of them have experience or resources that could help you? Put them at the top of the list!

3. Next, widen your circle a bit and think about adults you interact with regularly such as teachers, coaches, and pastors. If your venture involves music, for example, your piano teacher might be the perfect mentor. Add these people to your list.

4. Now, think about what specific kinds of skills your venture might need and what local businesspeople could offer those. Plan to sell custom-designed T-shirts online? You might want a professional artist on your team. Collecting books to stock a new library? Ask a librarian to get involved. Don't forget to consider retirees and senior citizens in your community. They might have the skills, connections, interest, and—perhaps most importantly—the time to lend some vital support when you need it. If any people come to mind here, put them on the list, too.

5. Alternatively, you can approach established organizations in your field to see if they have anyone available, like Charles did. Or, identify other young changemakers who've gone before you (such as the ones profiled in this book!) and see if they're interested. You can also try looking on Score.org—a nonprofit association dedicated to growing successful small businesses in the United States—or check out JuniorAchievement.org for a center in your area that might be able to match you with someone in your community. Add these ideas to the list.

6. Now go back over your list and number your mentor candidates in order of who you'd like to approach first.

When you're thinking about possible mentors, don't be afraid to aim high! Think about who your dream mentor would be, and then just step up and ask. There's no guarantee that person will say yes, but she may be able to connect you with someone who can. Or, maybe she'll be able to help in other ways, through a donation or an appearance at an event. And, you never know, she might just say yes!

You absolutely must have at least one committed adult mentor. In the chapters that follow, you'll see all the duties he can help you with—like writing a business plan, figuring out what kind of bank account to open, and reserving event space for your fundraisers. So keep going until you find someone who is willing to sign on. But there's no need to stop at just one, either! If you can think of several people who might be helpful in different areas, go ahead and ask them. Maybe you'll even be lucky enough to form a diverse board of advisors who can help you tackle all kinds of tough problems.

HOW TO APPROACH A POTENTIAL MENTOR

The odds of someone coming to you and asking if they can be your mentor are, sadly, almost zero. Fortunately, the odds of anyone you ask saying yes are good! Asking people to mentor you validates what they do and flatters them. The fact that you look up to them and are asking for their advice—not their money or another big investment—is usually enough to make them want to help.

Whomever you decide to approach, remember your elevator pitch and call to action from chapter 5. Explain to them what you're trying to do and why you care. Show them that you've already thought about how you'll go about doing it. Tell them what you think they can do to help. And ask them if they have more ideas.

Lisa Bardwell and her husband helped Charles learn how to lead people and think about organizational issues within his nonprofit. They expanded his knowledge about the environmental movement as a whole, and they discussed everything from history to biology to religion to life in general. Now, Charles says, they are like members of his family. Before you ask anyone to be your mentor, clarify for yourself and your potential adult mentor what exactly you hope her role will be . . . and what it won't be. An adult mentor is someone who can give you advice, connect you with other helpful adults or services, and offer encouragement throughout the process. But a mentor shouldn't make any decisions for you, take on any financial or legal risks on your behalf, or get directly involved in either the planning or running of your venture.

Take a few moments to write in your venture journal about your vision for your mentor's role. Be specific about what you want from your mentor. You might even want to type up your expectations and print them out so you can both sign that you understand them. This up-front communication will lay the groundwork for a successful long-term relationship. Here's an example of what a mentor agreement might look like:

MENTOR AGREEMENT

Mentor's Name: Bob Smith
Mentor's Email Address: bobsmith@email.com
Mentor's Mailing Address: 123 Elm Lane, Springfield
Mentor's Phone Number: 555-555-1212

Description of Mentor's Responsibilities and Commitments:
As a certified public accountant, Bob Smith agrees to advise Venture X on decisions related to bookkeeping and taxes to the best of his professional ability, not to exceed one hour per week and scheduled at Bob's convenience.

Signing this agreement indicates the Mentor understands the expectations set forth in this agreement and that the Mentor is committed to fulfilling those responsibilities to Venture X.

Mentor's Signature: _____ Date: _____

Venture X Leader's Signature: _____ Date: _____

In My Experience

Mentors are helpful to people of any age and with any endeavor, not just starting a social venture. When I started writing, I sought out mentors. It was hard because I felt like such a newbie, and it was embarrassing to admit what I didn't know. One thing I did know, though, was that the quickest way to learn and improve was to seek advice from the pros.

In my experience, when we want something badly enough to push ourselves outside our comfort zones and go for it, we are usually rewarded. I once called a hiring manager at home, on a Sunday, to explain how much I wanted the job he was offering, even though I knew he'd already filled the position. Anyone with enough courage to do that, he said, was someone he wanted on his team. He made a new position, and I got the job.

So, when I was desperate to take one of my manuscripts to the next level but didn't know how to do it, I pushed way outside of my comfort zone and asked one of my all-time favorite authors if she'd look at it for me. This wasn't just any author . . . she was a Newbery Honor winner and New York Times *bestselling author Kirby Larson.*

To my surprise, she said yes! Then, I was even more nervous. I would have to show her my work. What if she thought it was terrible and regretted her decision to help me? How could I have put such a nice person in such a terrible position? Always a class act, however, Kirby sent me back one of the best critiques I have ever received, along with a fair amount of much-needed encouragement.

I might have stopped writing if I hadn't found someone who could push me farther along the right path. At the very least, I would have been stuck in place much longer. I don't know if Kirby fully understood what it meant for me to reach out to her or for her to respond

the way she did, but I know I'll be forever grateful to her for offering the perfect guidance just when I needed it.

There's someone out there who can do the same for you. Find him or her, and just ask.

ADVISORS

A board of advisors is a group of adult professionals who help an organization by offering advice and expertise. This is different from a board of directors, which is the governing body of a corporation. Advisors are not paid employees or regular volunteers, but rather they are involved simply because they care about the mission and want to see it succeed. Your advisors won't be involved in the day-to-day getting-things-done part of your venture, but they can help you with big-picture planning and long-term strategies. You will probably want to schedule monthly or quarterly meetings with your board of advisors to go over what you've accomplished and lay out your ideas for what you're planning to do next.

Some important people to consider recruiting for your board of advisors are a lawyer, an accountant, and anyone with special knowledge of or experience in the problem you're trying to solve.

One word of warning: Your mentors and advisors might act encouraging and positive all of the time, no matter what the stakes are. You're a young person, after all, and you're trying to do good in the world. Who could say anything bad about that? You need them to do more than just play cheerleader, though. You need people who will tell it to you straight. Explain to them up front that you don't want to be treated like a kid. Tell them you are serious about making this venture work, about making a real impact on your issue, and that you are asking them for their honest advice. Assure them you are ready for some tough love. Then, really listen to what they have to say—even though it might not be easy for you to hear—and consider how you might apply it. Your venture will be better off in the long run.

IT'S STILL UP TO YOU

Remember that any mentor or advisor relationship is only going to be as useful as *you* make it. First, you have to be willing to actually reach out to those people with specific questions and to schedule open-ended discussion time. They've agreed to be your guides—use them! Second, don't necessarily do everything they tell you to. Always consider what they are saying and why, but if the advice still doesn't feel right, it's okay to not follow it.

As Charles says, "Heroes are just people who do what they can with what they have—so be who you are, using what you have, to make a difference."

Better than a thousand days of diligent study is one day with a great teacher.

Japanese Proverb

| 7 |

Meeting Magic

The great leader is not necessarily the one who does the greatest things; he is the one who gets the people to do the greatest things.

Ronald Reagan, 40th President of the United States,
as quoted by James Strock in *Reagan on Leadership:*
Executive Lessons from the Great Communicator

Every venture—whether it's a three-person club or a corporation with thousands of employees—needs meetings to keep everybody informed and working toward the same mission. When the big technology boom first began, people speculated that, in the future, everyone would work from home and there'd be no offices or business centers. Despite the many voice and video capabilities available today and the numerous ways to collaborate online cheaply and efficiently, that prediction still hasn't come to pass. Why not? Sometimes, face-to-face is still the best way to communicate and the fastest way to make decisions.

Meetings can be a great way to brainstorm ideas, share information, answer questions, solve problems, make decisions, or create a plan. If they accomplish those things, your team meetings will be successful and rewarding experiences for everyone. If they don't, the meetings will be frustrating wastes of everyone's time. Luckily, there are some easy ways to make sure all of your meetings are productive. This chapter will help.

GIRLS TALK, CODMAN SQUARE NEIGHBORHOOD DEVELOPMENT CORPORATION

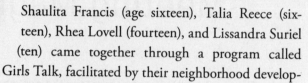

Shaulita Francis (age sixteen), Talia Reece (sixteen), Rhea Lovell (fourteen), and Lissandra Suriel (ten) came together through a program called Girls Talk, facilitated by their neighborhood development corporation in Codman Square, Massachusetts. Under the program's facilitator, Danielle Smith, the girls were to come up with and plan a social venture that would improve their neighborhood. They had noticed that there was a lot of litter throughout the community and that many of their neighbors just threw their trash anywhere. So, the four decided to take on the cause of promoting a cleaner neighborhood. "We wanted to feel proud of our community and where we live," Talia says.

The girls pledged to do a better job themselves and to educate others to follow their lead. But how? Their first challenge was figuring out what to do. They wanted to find a product they could sell that would raise money as well as raising awareness. They had many meetings, brainstormed ideas together, and took several votes to narrow it down to just one: selling custom-printed reusable tumblers and using the profits to sponsor trash cans in key areas of the community.

Learning how to be a part of an effective team was one of the best things about launching a venture, Shaulita says. Rhea agrees, adding that her favorite benefits were improved communication skills and the experience of working with other people. The girls gained other things along the way, too. Rhea became more comfortable speaking in public. Talia says she gained better planning skills and is more organized. And Lissandra learned to keep trying even when things get difficult.

And things did get tough! Still, the team kept going. Sometimes the team just got off track or needed a break, and they were grateful to have their mentor help them get back in line. They all felt compelled to stick it out so they could say they had done something important for their neighborhood. And once they had set an event date and publicized it, they didn't want to cancel and disappoint people who were looking forward to it.

WHEN AND WHERE?

Assuming at least some of your meetings will be face-to-face, you'll need to think about when and where to have them. It's okay if not everyone on the team can be at every meeting, but try to schedule the meetings so that most of the core team members can attend. It might help to hold the meetings on a regular day and time—every Friday at lunchtime, for example, or on the first Tuesday of every month—so members can plan ahead and make sure they are free at those times.

Where to have the meetings depends on how many people will attend, where they'll be coming from, and the space available. If your parents approve, you may be able to hold meetings at your house. The school might also be a natural choice, especially if all of your team members attend the same school. Another option is a public meeting place such as a library conference room, which can often be reserved in advance for free. Restaurants and coffee shops can work great for these types of meetings, too. Be sure to consider the size of the group, the location of the space, its size, the available features (for example, will you need electrical outlets or a whiteboard?), and the noise level—of your group and of the space. You want your group to work for the space as much as you want the space to work for you!

BREAKING THE ICE

If your team members don't already know each other, starting out with a fun icebreaker can be a great way to put everyone at ease while getting acquainted. Icebreakers are simple games meant to encourage people to share or mingle. Here are a few to try:

TAKE AS MUCH AS YOU NEED

1. Use any item that has lots of pieces and is inexpensive, like candy, toilet paper, pennies, or chocolate chips. Pass it around the group.

2. Tell your team members only, "Take as much as you think you will need." Don't tell them what it's for!

3. After the participants have taken their items, tell them that for each piece they took, they must share something about themselves with the team.

If you wish, you can assign categories to different colored items. For example, yellow candies might mean people have to tell something personal about themselves, red might mean they have to tell why they joined the team, and green might mean they have to say something they're good at.

POSTER IT

1. Bring in a big sheet of poster board, markers, old magazines, scissors, and glue.

2. Have your team members work together to create a collage poster about what the venture means to them, why they decided to join the team, or what they hope the venture will accomplish.

You can restrict it to only pictures, only words, or a free mixture of both.

TWO TRUTHS AND A LIE

1. Have each person, including yourself, write down three statements about him- or herself. Two of the statements must be true, but the other must be a lie.

2. After everyone has written down three statements, have one person read all three of his statements aloud in random order.

3. The rest of the team must then guess which one is the lie.

4. After the correct answer is revealed, the next person reads her statements aloud, and so on.

It is helpful if you go first as a demonstration before team members write their statements. Once they understand how the game works, they'll be more creative at coming up with surprising truths to share!

BEANBAG TOSS

1. First, have team members form the smallest circle possible.

2. If your team members don't know each other's names yet, instruct whoever has the beanbag (or stuffed toy, ball, orange, or other throwable object) to say his own name and then throw the item to someone else in the circle.

3. He then takes a step back.

4. The next person says her own name, throws the item to someone else still in the inside circle, and steps back.

5. When everyone in the small circle has said his or her name and stepped back, start over again.

6. If you run out of space or get too far apart to throw the item, start over in the center again.

7. When everyone has said his or her own name once or twice, switch to calling out the name of the person you are going to throw to instead of your own name.

8. Continue until you think everyone knows everyone else's name.

You can also have people say something about themselves instead of their names, or have them offer someone else a compliment instead of just saying the person's name.

ALL MY FRIENDS

1. Designate a leader to start the game. Have him stand on one side of the room, and the team members stand on the other.

2. The leader starts by saying, "All my friends . . ." and filling in something that applies to himself.

3. Everyone on the team who agrees with that statement for themselves takes one step forward.

4. The leader continues coming up with "All my friends . . ." statements until someone gets close enough to touch him. The first person to touch the leader gets to be the new leader, and the game starts over.

For example, the leader might say, "All my friends like to read." If all but two of the team members like to read, everyone would take a step forward except those two. Next, the leader says, "All my friends love cats." Three team members love cats—including one of the people who didn't like to read—so those three all step forward. The leader then says, "All my friends know how to swim." Five team members step forward, and one is able to touch the leader. She becomes the new leader.

ALLOW ME TO INTRODUCE YOU

1. Have the team split up into two equal groups, Group A and Group B.

2. Give each member of Group A a pen and some paper.

3. Then have each member of Group A pair up with a member from Group B.

4. Have each Group A member interview his or her Group B partner. Give everyone a set amount of time to ask questions and record the answers (around two minutes).

5. Then, have the partners switch roles so the Group B team members interview their Group A partners. Give them the same amount of time to ask questions and record the answers.

6. Finally, have everyone report what they learned about their partners to the rest of the group.

It's often much easier, and more interesting, to introduce other people than it is to introduce ourselves!

Try searching online for "meeting icebreakers" if you want to find even more ideas. Even after your team members know each other, doing some kind of bonding activity at the beginning of each meeting can keep your team interested in working together and having fun.

In My Experience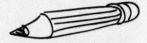

The advisory committee for SCBWI Western Washington always starts meetings by having each person share something new about him- or herself. Since we're all writers, it's usually either the best books we've read recently or what writing projects we're currently working on. We have almost twenty members, so going around the room to do this takes quite a bit of time.

When I first started with SCBWI, I thought that time was wasted. I was used to the corporate world and just wanted to get down to business. However, I soon realized that the introduction time was vital to the long-term health of our all-volunteer organization. First, it gave us a way to reconnect since we sometimes went months without a face-to-face meeting. Second, it gave us all a window into each other's personalities and helped us get to know each other better. Third, it gave us something more personal to talk about outside of the meetings, which brought us all together as friends.

Even though we work in fairly autonomous roles and don't necessarily see each other often, we've developed a close personal bond. I consider the people who serve on that committee with me to be my closest friends. Most of us continue volunteering for years, if not decades. That kind of commitment and stability is a key factor in the organization's ongoing success. And I think those first "wasted" minutes of every meeting are largely responsible.

MEETING MUSTS

Now that your team members are acquainted, it's time to get down to business. There are a few key ingredients to holding successful meetings. You and your secretary can work together to make sure these tasks get done.

NAME TAGS

If people don't know each other well, make name tags for everyone to wear and start with one of the icebreakers from the previous section to help make your team members feel comfortable with each other.

AGENDAS

Before every meeting, send out an agenda to everyone on the team. Your agenda will specify the time and place for the meeting, state the meeting's purpose, list what you hope to have accomplished by the end of the meeting, and present your plan for getting there. Think of the agenda as your outline or road map for the meeting. Creating an agenda will make running the meeting itself much easier for you, because it forces you to think about the meeting ahead of time.

Here's a sample agenda:

AGENDA: VENTURE TEAM MEETING

Saturday, May 14, 3:00–5:00 PM at Laurie's house

Purpose: We need a name for our venture.

Goal: At the end of the meeting, we'll have a name that the whole team can agree on.

Plan:
Team introductions/icebreaker (3:00–3:15)
Brainstorming session (3:15–3:45)
Discuss options and identify top contenders (3:45–4:15)
Vote (4:15–4:20)
Discussion and final consensus (4:20–4:50)
Cookies! (4:50–5:00)

In addition to helping you plan, sending the agenda out before the meeting will help your team members think about their roles and how they can contribute to the purpose at hand. It also allows your team members to point out things you might not have thought about so you can revise the agenda if necessary. You may even want to assign a task for your team members to complete before the meeting. In the example above, you could ask everyone to come prepared to share two name suggestions to get the brainstorming session started.

Keep your meetings as short as possible, and try to stick to one purpose at a time so things don't get overwhelming and out of control. Remember that your agenda is only a guideline. If you find things go more quickly or take longer than you thought they would, that's okay. Refer to your agenda as necessary to stay on track, but be flexible enough to set new goals if the meeting calls for it.

ACTION ITEMS

During most meetings, things will come up that need to be done by someone after the meeting is over, and team members will volunteer to do those tasks. Make sure someone keeps track of these action items as they are discussed. Then, at the end of the meeting, read all of the action items to remind each team member exactly what is expected of him or her.

VOTING

A word about voting . . . sometimes it's easiest to take a quick vote and go with the majority. Other times (such as the naming example above) you should make sure everyone is on board with a decision and have the team reach a consensus. Trust your judgment on which kind of decision you're facing, how it will affect the team, and whether or not voting is appropriate.

MINUTES

Have your secretary (or a designated temporary secretary) keep a record of everything that happens during the meeting, and send these notes out to the whole team as soon as possible. This helps make sure nobody misses or forgets what the team discussed in the meeting and keeps everyone on the team in sync.

STANDARD OPERATING PROCEDURE

If you've ever watched a formal meeting take place, such as a city council or school board meeting, you've probably heard lots of special phrases like *making a motion*, *old business*, *new business*, and *all in favor*. Those keywords and the rules that go with them—known as parliamentary procedure—are used to make meetings with lots of different kinds of people easier for everyone to participate in.

You probably won't need to be quite that rigid with your venture team meetings, but it will still help to have a basic template to plan your meeting agendas around. Here's a proposed parliamentary procedure for your venture team meetings:

1. **Opening:** This part of the meeting is for introductions, icebreakers, welcome, announcements, good news, and friendly sharing on a personal topic relevant to all. It should be a short, casual way to come together as people and re-establish relationships.

2. **Old business:** This part of the meeting might include reports from various team members about their activities since the last meeting as well as any necessary follow-up regarding unfinished topics from previous meetings.

3. **New business:** This is the main part of the meeting, where you address the purpose of the meeting and work to achieve the meeting's goal.

4. **Wrap-up:** This is where you take any necessary votes, state the outcome of the meeting, and read off any action items to be completed after the meeting. End by thanking your team members for coming and sending them off on an encouraging note.

UNMEETINGS

Of course, sometimes it just isn't practical to get everyone together in the same room, and one of the biggest advantages your generation has over previous ones is technology. The virtual connectedness you have to one another plus the number of digital tools available to you nearly 24/7 means you don't have to hold a physical meeting in order to get work done.

You can have virtual meetings using conference call services, chats, and video sharing tools like Skype or Google Hangouts. These kinds of tools allow you to get together with your team conveniently, often for free, whether you're across town or around the world from each other. It's not the same as meeting face-to-face, of course, but it can save you some hassle and be an effective alternative.

You also have access to things like Google Drive, Dropbox, and other online services for sharing and collaborating on different kinds of documents, as well as things like Trello for basic project management functionality. Tools like these can greatly increase your team's productivity while saving you countless hours, so they're worth exploring if you're not already familiar with them.

Remember, though, that even with all of this great technology at your disposal, getting people together and sharing common experiences is an important element of team building, which adds to the long-term stability of your team—and increases the fun you can have!

LAST WORDS OF WISDOM

The Girls Talk team said that voting on issues and finding ideas that everyone was happy with were some of their biggest challenges. They agreed, though, that learning how to communicate with each other and working as a team were some of the most valuable rewards gained from their collaborative venture experience.

As the leader, it is up to you to encourage everyone's participation, respect their opinions, and acknowledge their contributions during your team meetings. As Shaulita says, "Communicate with everybody in the group so everybody's on the same page." To do that, remember that some people may be more comfortable speaking in a group, while others may need to be specifically asked for their opinions before they're willing to share them. And, of course, as Rhea adds, "Have fun with it!"

> One of the most profound things I've learned as a Grown Up is how few people it takes to change the world forever.
>
> Maggie Stiefvater, *New York Times* bestselling author, on Twitter and Facebook, May 8, 2013

| 8 |

Business Planning 101

If we all did the things we are capable of doing, we would literally astound ourselves.

Often attributed to Thomas Edison, inventor and businessman

One of the first things your team will need to tackle in your meetings is the business plan. Regardless of where your venture falls on the profit/nonprofit spectrum or how formalized your business structure is or isn't, it's worth the effort to make a strong business plan.

For many entrepreneurs, it's tempting to skip this step of formalizing your plan and just jump right in. After all, you've found your passion, you have an idea you're excited about, and you have a team of people ready to go . . . why wait, right? Well, if you want to be successful, not waste other people's time and money (not to mention your own!), and actually solve that problem you identified in chapter 3, you'd better have a solid plan for how you're going to go about it before you make the next move. Taking the time to draft a business plan will help you get your thoughts organized, maximize your team's efforts and impact, and show others that you're serious and capable. And that can lead to additional volunteers, new mentors, bigger donations, better grants, extra media attention, stronger partnerships, and more!

Now that you have your team in place and know how to run effective meetings, you can all work together to draft your business plan. Be sure to involve the whole team in this process so everyone knows the plan inside and out and can commit to it 100 percent. Don't worry, though. It won't be as hard as you might think. We'll break it down step by step.

Profile

TEAM aWEARness, TRANSITION HOUSE

Team aWEARness had a different beginning than most of the ventures profiled so far. In this rather unusual case, the team—Natnale Mengesha, Amira Nwokeji-Iwuala, Jonathan Rosario, Christian Abebe, Lidwine St. Rose, and Keshena Octavien—came together through an innovative program called Youth Action Corps, which hires local youth to undertake community improvement projects. Youth Action Corps operates on behalf of Transition House, an agency in Cambridge, Massachusetts, that focuses on reducing domestic and teen dating violence in the community by providing emergency shelter, transitional and supported housing, and youth prevention education. Despite the fact that they came from different schools and neighborhoods and their issue was assigned to them, the team members came together, set goals, assigned roles, refined their mission, and developed a detailed, original venture plan in just a few short months with the help of their mentor, Zohar Fuller.

Jonathan told the team about another project he had seen on the television show *The Real World—San Diego*, where Nate Stodghill partnered with Flex watches to raise awareness of suicide and launch a website to encourage discussion of the issue (TheLivingMemoir.com). Inspired by that effort, Team aWEARness decided to make bracelets and create a blog that focused on domestic and teen dating violence. Once they had their idea nailed down, the team members put together a plan.

They identified goals and broke each of those goals down into the discrete steps it would take to complete them. Then, they worked out a detailed month-by-month schedule of how the team would proceed toward each goal. That allowed them to see that the project was manageable.

"The timeline was the easiest part of the plan for me," says Lidwine. "I'm an organized person, and I like to do things according to each month. Once we had the information, the timeline was really fast."

They also needed to decide who would do each of those steps. Fortunately, they found that they all had at least one area of interest or expertise that could add to the team, so they volunteered for the roles that suited them best. Natnale was good with computers and technology, so he became the blog manager. Jonathan and Christian were creative and wanted to head up the bracelet design and assembly. Lidwine and Keshena were good at persuading people to do things, so they became the managers of advertising, responsible for designing and making the flyers. And Amira became the manager of sales, keeping track of the budget and everything related to the team's finances.

The team members pooled their knowledge and research to develop a precise budget showing how much it would cost to buy materials for the bracelets, host the website, distribute flyers, and get to events to spread the word. They also calculated how much money they would need to raise through grants, donations, and bracelet sales to cover those expenses. Jonathan felt that this was the hardest part of the plan, but also the most important. "Without the budget, we wouldn't have been able to do anything," he says. "The budget made us think about it more in depth."

With all of their planning in place, the team was ready to get to work. They checked in with their plan often to track their progress, and when the time came they were ready with three hundred bracelets to sell, decorative bags to put them in, custom messages to place inside, and a blog where bracelet purchasers could go to post their own stories about interpersonal violence, ask questions, or offer support to victims (awearness-yac.tumblr.com).

The team successfully took part in several community events selling bracelets, raising money, showcasing their blog, and—most importantly—raising awareness of and starting a discussion about their issue. Together, they took an important step in reducing domestic and dating violence in their community.

BUSINESS PLAN BASICS

A business plan is really just a written explanation of your goals, your plans to achieve those goals, and how you intend to handle the money coming in and going out as you do so. Over time, you will probably develop different business plans for different audiences. Investors, donors, and organizations offering grant money may require an application in the form of a detailed, sophisticated business plan. And, of course, as your venture grows and changes, your business plan will need to be updated to reflect your new goals. For now, though, your main audience is you and your team, and you can start with the basics. At this stage, your business plan should include:

1. Your venture's name

2. A description of your venture

3. Your short- and long-term goals for the venture

4. The roles and responsibilities of everyone involved with the venture

5. The venture's current budget and financial plans for the future

Let's take a look at these sections one by one.

Take notes in your venture journal to keep track of your thoughts and ideas while you read this chapter, and hold team meetings as necessary to discuss the different sections.

STEP 1: THE NAME

The first thing you need is a name. Names are important—often they're the first impression your venture will make on someone. Take your time to brainstorm lots of ideas. There are a few questions to keep in mind:

1. Is the domain name available? You'll probably want a website sooner or later, and you need to make sure the URL you want isn't already taken by somebody else. When you find a domain name, grab it as soon as possible on a service like Name.com or NameCheap.com. It's easy and inexpensive, and doing this early will save you head-aches later.

2. Does anyone have the name trademarked already? You can do a search using the Trademark Electronic Search System provided by the United States Patent and Trademark Office. It costs money and takes time to file for a trademark, so you probably don't need to rush out and do it for yourself right now. You do want to make sure you're not infringing on someone else's trademark, though.

3. Does the name have the right meaning? Does it convey what your venture is and does? Are there any alternative meanings that could lead to a potential misunderstanding, or worse yet, a turnoff? Check the dictionary—and an online urban dictionary and perhaps some translators—to make sure you're not saying something you didn't intend!

4. Is it readable and writable? If people can't pronounce it, they won't want to talk about it. If they can't spell it, they won't be able to write about it (or search for it).

5. Does it sound good? You don't want to cringe every time you hear it, and you don't want supporters to, either.

One of my favorite blogs is Christopher Johnson's The Name Inspector (TheNameInspector.com). Check it out for a witty and entertaining analysis of some well-known, and not-so-well-known, company names. As the about page says, "The Name Inspector takes a close look at names and tells you what makes them tick—or tank." Then ask yourself: Would my venture name pass The Name Inspector's test?

STEP 2: THE DESCRIPTION

The description will act as the introduction to your venture. Think of it as a broad overview, intended to give the background and reasoning behind the rest of the plans in later sections. This is your chance to ground readers in your big idea and share some glimpses of your passion and research from chapters 3 and 4, and it's an expansion on the elevator pitch you wrote in chapter 5.

The first things people looking at your venture will want to know are:

- What is your idea?

- What problem is your venture trying to solve?

- Who will be your venture's customers or clients?

- What difference will your venture make?

- Why is your venture necessary?

You've already figured most of this out for yourself in the previous chapters, so it should be fairly easy to reuse the work you've done so far, especially since you've kept good notes in your venture journal. Talk about the problem you've identified, the research you've already done to learn about it (including any compelling statistics you found), and how you plan to solve it. Explain exactly what led you and your team to address this issue. Give a brief overview of how you're going to do it, but save the details for later. This first section should focus on two Ws: *why* you're launching this particular venture and *what* your venture is going to do.

STEP 3: GOALS

The goals section gets into the *how* of your venture. You can think of it as two separate parts: short-term goals and long-term goals. Short-term goals are the immediate actions—more of a to-do list—that will guide your venture toward its long-term goals—or bigger hopes and dreams. Whatever type of goals they are, you want to make sure they're SMART goals.

SMART Goals

SMART is an acronym used to help people remember how to develop strong, meaningful goals. SMART goals are:

- **S**pecific: Your goals should be specific enough that anyone, especially people from outside of your team, can look at them and understand what you're trying to do and how you plan to do it.

- **M**easurable: There should be an easy way to tell if you've met each goal or not. How will you define success?

- **A**ctionable: Is there a clear series of steps that you can take to achieve each of your goals? Be sure to include what the steps are and in what order you will take them.

- **R**ealistic: Your goals must be reasonable given the resources you have available. Can you really do what you're planning?

- **T**imely: Your goals should have clear beginning and end dates.

Learn to check your goals against each of the SMART components and you'll have a much better chance of success.

Short-Term Goals

Your business plan should have three or four clear, attainable goals that will drive your venture's immediate next steps. Think of these as the big items on your current to-do list. Especially since you're just starting out, it's helpful to think of short-term goals as ways of testing your big idea—with the least amount of effort and risk possible. You wouldn't want to launch a major initiative just to find out it had a fatal flaw, right? So, start by breaking your overall idea into pieces and thinking about how you can test each one.

Let's look at an example. Say your idea is to print your team's original artwork on T-shirts, which you'll then sell to raise money, which you'll use to buy new school clothes for foster children. There are three major pieces there—printing, selling, and donating—and you should test each of them in some small way before going all out. In this case, your short-term goals may be:

1. In the next two weeks, decide the best way to print original art on a T-shirt by researching the different options: doing it ourselves, uploading it to an online service, or taking it to a local printing company.

2. By December, make ten T-shirts and try selling them at several different places and times to see what works best.

3. Before the end of the month, find one organization to partner with that helps foster children and will be happy to accept our donations.

You can see that each of these goals is SMART: specific, measurable, actionable, realistic, and timely. If you simply said, "Get shirts made, sell them, and give the money to foster children," that wouldn't be specific, measurable, or timely.

You'll have to spend some time carefully defining and refining your goals until you get them just right. Have your team help with this process to ensure everyone agrees with the final goal statements.

Long-Term Goals

In addition to your short-term goals, you also need to demonstrate that you've given some thought to what your venture will look like down the road, both in terms of actions and in terms of people.

First, think about what big goals you are building up to beyond the short-term goals. What do you hope your venture will be doing one year from now? How about five years from now? Don't be afraid to go big here. If you have a grand vision, this is the perfect place to capture and share it. And, it's also the first step toward making it a reality!

Sometimes it's helpful to start with your long-term goals and work backward to the short-term goals. You might want to create a report written in the imagined future, reflecting on the accomplishments you've achieved at that point. Or, write a "letter from the founder"—dated ten years in the future—which thanks your biggest donors and partners and outlines the dream successes their support helped you achieve. These future dreams are your long-term goals. The steps you can take toward them—right now—are your short-term goals.

STEP 4: PEOPLE

The next section of your business plan is all about the people involved: you, team members, volunteers, allies, mentors, and advisors.

First, list everyone on your team—including yourself—and the role or roles that each person is currently responsible for. Briefly mention why each team member was chosen for each role and what skills make him or her suitable for the role. Refer to your notes from chapter 5 as well as the formal summary you gave everyone when you were assembling your team. You want to show that you have a strong, full team made up of passionate, committed, and capable individuals who have the energy, skills, and integrity to succeed. Again, make sure everyone on your team is aware of and agrees on this list!

Next, list any adults who are going to help you and what services they will provide. Use your notes from chapter 6 as well as the text from your mentor agreement to help you write this part.

Finally, explain how you plan to maintain the necessary volunteers, team members, and leadership so your venture will continue to thrive. Doing a one-time or short-term project has its benefits, of course—both for you and for the community—but real changemakers and social entrepreneurs think longer term. They build ongoing solutions to problems and thus maximize their impact and minimize the problem. Try to set up your venture so that it can grow and become a lasting organization for the future, whether or not you stay with the organization when you graduate high school, go to college, take other jobs, or start a family.

STEP 5: MONEY

The money section of your plan will detail your budget—where you plan to find the money you need to get started and keep your venture going, and how you plan to use that money to achieve your goals. If you're going to ask anyone for money—whether it's donations, loans, or grants—you will need to show them how you plan to use it. And if you're going to raise money—through sales, services, or events—you will need to know how much to charge so you will make money instead of losing it!

Expenses

There are two kinds of expenses: start-up costs and operating expenses. Start-up costs are just that, the one-time expenses necessary just to get your venture off the ground. Maybe you need a new printer to print out flyers, or perhaps your county requires you to get a special license before you can work with food. Think about everything you need to get your idea off the ground. If it's a special one-time item, put it in the start-up costs category.

Your operating costs are the ongoing expenses that you'll have to pay regularly in order to keep your venture humming along. This might mean buying enough yarn to knit those forty hats the homeless shelter needs each month or the fees for renting a room at the local community center to teach dance classes. Some of your operating costs will be fixed, meaning you'll pay the same thing regardless of your activities (such as website hosting). Other operating costs are variable, meaning they will change every time (such as how many bracelets you make for your next event, which will vary depending on the type of event it is). It's also helpful to think about which costs are discretionary—meaning you could choose to eliminate them if necessary, like having cookies at your meetings—and which ones aren't, like paying your taxes.

Income

Knowing how much money you can expect to come in down the road will help you plan for how your venture can grow! In the income section, you'll try to predict your venture's expected income from all available sources like donations, grants, product or ticket sales, or other payments received. You need to make sure your income will be at least as high as your expenses. But, because you have more expenses in the beginning of a venture—before you've started receiving any income—it can be hard to get your idea off the ground. Chapter 10 has specific how-tos for getting different kinds of income, but for now, just make some guesses for how much you can realistically expect. Then, come back and fine-tune your plan as you learn more in later chapters.

PUTTING IT ALL TOGETHER

Now, go back and look over all of the notes you've taken in your journal related to your venture's business plan, as well as the minutes from all of the team meetings where you discussed business plan ideas. Put it all together into the five-step outline previously explained, similar to the following plan that Team aWEARness made. When you have it all worked out, type it up as a formal document and save it for future reference.

BUSINESS PLAN: TEAM aWEARNESS

Name: Team aWEARness: Speak Your Mind, You're Not Alone

Description: Our idea is to raise awareness and discussion about domestic violence and teen dating violence by creating a blog and selling bracelets that symbolize the different types of abuse. The blog is going to have different stories and thoughts submitted by survivors of domestic violence and anyone who has a question or a comment about the topic. Anyone will be able to submit a story or question to the blog, and we will post answers and resources. We will also lead educational workshops about dating violence where teens can come and learn more about the topic, and they can make their own bracelets that they can keep for free.

We were inspired to make and sell these bracelets by someone who did a similar project creating and distributing watches to raise awareness for suicide. That project gave the chance for people to learn and talk about how significant suicide is. We think that bracelets are a unique and popular way of introducing an important subject matter to teens, because we know that teenagers love and notice each other's jewelry every day. Since teens are not that aware of the different types of abuse and should learn about them, these bracelets give an interesting way to do that. We wanted to make the blog because we know that teens spend a lot of time online, and since it is online people will get to read it from all over the country and beyond.

This would get teens in our community starting to become aware of dating and domestic violence. It would let them know how serious an issue it is. When people notice the bracelets, it will make them question why people are wearing them, and that will start a conversation about the topic. They will then be able to go online to the blog for a chance to learn more about the topic and ask questions. The blog also supplies support to survivors in our community and a voice to express what they might not be able to in person. We will know if we are successful if many people all over school start buying and wearing the bracelets and start asking each other questions about domestic violence. We will also know we're successful if people start knowing about us and what we do, so that they can join if they want or they can come to us as a resource. Another indicator of success would be if a lot of people show up at our educational workshops. As for our blog, we will be able to see how many views we get and if people are mentioning us on Twitter and liking us on Facebook.

3. Goals:

Goal #1: Make three hundred domestic violence awareness bracelets to sell over six months at schools, public events, and community centers. This will involve purchasing materials, making bracelets, advertising (wearing them and launching an ad campaign), and establishing a sales system.

Goal #2: Educate purchasers in the community about domestic violence issues by attaching facts to bracelet package. This will involve creating messages tailored to the bracelets, purchasing materials for messages, putting messages in gift bags with bracelets, and telling our customers about the messages.

Goal #3: Facilitate community discussion by leading educational workshops and creating the domestic violence blog that highlights individual stories, facts, and questions. To achieve this, we'll need to create a blog template, create initial blog content, advertise the blog, manage the website, and lead educational workshops at schools and other youth groups.

4. People:

NAME	ROLE	RESPONSIBILITY
Christian	Bracelet Designer & Comanager	Design the bracelets, get materials for the bracelets, help manage the making of the bracelets by explaining to others how to make them and determine which events people should be creating bracelets at
Jonathan	Bracelet Designer & Comanager	Design the bracelets, get materials for the bracelets, help manage the making of the bracelets by explaining to others how to make them and determine which events people should be creating bracelets at
Natnale	Blog Manager	Pick a blog template, advertise the blog around the school/community, put up the initial blog content, and be the lead person to collect online submissions
Lidwine	Comanager of Advertising	Design the flyers for bracelets and blog, design the messages that will be attached to the bracelets, purchase the flyers and messages, assemble the messages with the bracelets in the gift bags, put up the flyers around the community
Keshena	Comanager of Advertising	Design the flyers for bracelets and blog, design the messages that will be attached to the bracelets, purchase the flyers and messages, assemble the messages with the bracelets in the gift bags, put up the flyers around the community
Amira	Manager of Sales	Determine price for bracelets, determine a way to receive sales on the blog, keep track of records, determine where the profit of the bracelets will go

5. Budget:

(Note: In this case, the team had no startup costs, so their sample budget includes only operational expenses.)

Income

SOURCE OF INCOME	AMOUNT OF INCOME ($)	WHEN IS THIS EXPECTED? (MONTH)	COMMENTS
Youth Venture seed funding	791	December	
Fundraising events	200	August	
Revenue from bracelet purchases	400	Starting in April	
Donations from stores	150	September	
TOTAL FIRST-YEAR INCOME:	$1,541		

Expenses

SUPPLIES / EXPENSES	COST ONE ($)	NUMBER NEEDED (#)	TOTAL (COST OF ONE MULTIPLIED BY NUMBER NEEDED)	WHEN WILL THESE BE NEEDED? (MONTH)	GOAL
Flyers	(Set price for buying in bulk)	250	250.41	Half will be needed by February, other half by July	Advertising blog and bracelets
Bracelet Message Tags	(Set price for buying in bulk)	300	51.95	January	Educating purchasers about domestic violence and our blog
Bracelet Bags	$5 for 12	300	141.99 (includes s+h)	January	Distributing bracelets
Bracelet Thread	$2.00 for one roll + $3.50 shipping and $0.65 for s+h for each additional roll	24	66.45	January	Creating bracelets
Charms	$0.58	300	174	January	Attaching to the bracelets
Blog	$2.85/month	12 months	34.20	January	Creation and monthly fees for keeping the blog running
Transportation	$4 for each person to get to and from one workshop	18	72	March–July	Getting to workshops and events that we lead
TOTAL FIRST-YEAR EXPENSES:			**$791**		

In My Experience

I've served on several selection panels for Ashoka's Youth Venture, an organization dedicated to inspiring, investing in, and supporting young changemakers and their social ventures. At a selection panel

presentation, youth teams with venture ideas pitch their plans to a group of adults, who then decide which teams should receive funding for the ventures and how much. Their ventures' fates are, essentially, in our hands. Talk about nerve-wracking!

I always feel kind of sorry for the teens when they walk in and see us adults sitting in a line at the front of the room, watching them and waiting for them to start their pitches. The teams usually look pretty nervous—who wouldn't?

And then, always, the teens blow my mind! They come in with complete, well thought-out plans like the one above. They have polished presentations. They give detailed answers to our questions. They have done the work, they know what they're talking about, and their passion for their projects shines through in every word.

They're not always perfect, of course. There are usually a few suggestions we adults can offer, some additions the young changemakers could make to expand or strengthen their plans. But every single time I've participated, I've walked away from the experience feeling good about the world and where we're headed. If those teens can put together mind-blowing venture plans, so can you, and that gives me hope for the future. Start with a good plan, and let that plan take you to great places.

A PLAN IS JUST A PLAN

Remember, just because you've put all of this work and thought into your business plan doesn't mean it's now set in stone. You will need to adapt and revise your plan constantly to reflect new ideas, new information, and your venture's growth. Don't be afraid to deviate from the plan and modify it as needed to do what's right for your venture. Your business plan is a helpful tool, like a map, but you may discover other, better paths you didn't know about when you drew it up.

Team aWEARness found this out firsthand. They discovered that their original bracelet design took a long time to produce, and they weren't able to meet their goal of making three hundred bracelets before June. They went back to the drawing board over the summer, redesigned the bracelets to streamline production, and are now well on their way.

Plan everything your venture does, just like Team aWEARness did. Then act on your plan, evaluate how it went, and adjust the plan as necessary for the next time. You can think of this as an endlessly repeating cycle: plan, do, check, adjust, repeat. Nobody gets everything right the first time, and this process will help you learn from your mistakes so you can continually improve.

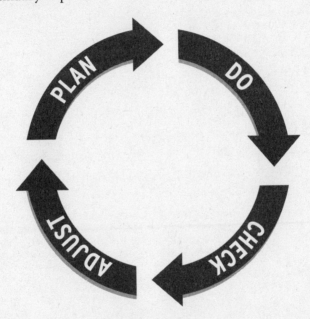

We do not need magic to transform our world. We carry all the power we need inside ourselves already: we have the power to imagine better.

J. K. Rowling, worldwide bestselling author, in the Harvard University commencement address on June 5, 2008

| 9 |
Money Matters

**Make the money,
don't let the money make you.**

Macklemore and Ryan Lewis in their song "Make the Money"

You're going to be handling money, so you need to have a plan for making and spending it and a system to keep track of it all. Your venture's treasurer is mainly in charge of this, but you need to know how to do it too so you can help each other. To some people that might sound boring or even a little bit intimidating, but what could be more fun than watching money roll in—money you helped earn—and using it to make the world a better place? It isn't that hard, and once you learn how, keeping track of money is a skill that will come in handy throughout your lifetime.

As Divine Bradley told the *Biz Kids* television program, "Young people need to know about money: not only how to work for it, but how to make money work for themselves." This chapter will introduce you to budgets, banking, and other financial issues, and give you the tools and knowledge to handle them like a pro.

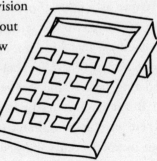

YOUTH ULTIMATE PROJECT

In the spring of 2010, a group of seniors visited Cambodia on a trip with their high school, The Northwest School in Seattle, Washington. They fell in love with the people and culture of Cambodia, but they saw one huge problem. There weren't enough schools, so the children living in Phnom Penh went to school for only half the day. When they weren't in school, they had nothing to do and were more likely to get into trouble.

Christopher Trinh, then a junior at The Northwest School, had seen that type of educational inequity on a trip to Vietnam with his family in 2009. With four of the seniors, he decided to try to solve the problem. Chris was active on his high school's ultimate Frisbee team, so he knew sports could be a positive outlet. He says playing ultimate Frisbee taught him perseverance, the meaning of hard work, and how to be responsible for a team. Since it had been such a worthwhile use of his time, he figured it would also be good for the children in Cambodia.

Chris and his friends got started as soon as they returned home, working to host fundraisers, win grants, and secure a sponsorship from local companies. By the following summer, they were back in Phnom Penh, but this time they were hosting free camps for kids that used ultimate Frisbee as a vehicle to teach character and life lessons. Chris says it's pretty simple to get started as a changemaker. You just need to find something that you love, and you can always find a way to turn that into helping others. It's about believing you have something that's worth sharing, he says, and that you can do it.

But it can be stressful, too. "When Youth Ultimate Project started, there were many unknowns and possibilities for failure," he says. For an inexperienced youth-led team with almost zero funds, there was always something to worry about—usually related to money. What if they didn't break even at the auction? What if they didn't get the grant? What would they do if they didn't have enough funding in time for the spring trip? "I quickly learned that I could not allow myself to dwell on the what-ifs," he says. "Instead, I stayed calm, cultivated a positive mind-set, and focused my attention on the things I could control."

But Chris says the rewards outweigh the challenges. "When things get tough, I remind myself who I am doing it for," he says. "If even just one camper makes the same connection I did and applies the values learned from ultimate Frisbee to his or her life, then it is worth it for me."

BUDGET: PLANNING WHAT MIGHT HAPPEN

As mentioned in chapter 8, a budget is really just a plan for the money going out of your venture, called expenses, and the money coming into your venture, called income. You already have an initial budget from your business plan. Start with that, and simply update it as you continue with your venture. Just like any plan, it won't be perfect, but the more accurately you can predict your expenses and income, the better off you'll be later.

Once you have a budget in place, you can more easily adapt your plans as needed and see the effects. "I've learned that it helps to plan and write everything down to the last detail," Chris says, "but it is also important to remember that not everything will go as planned, so having the ability to adapt is critical to being successful."

BOOKKEEPING: TRACKING WHAT DID HAPPEN

As soon as you pay for anything related to your venture or raise any money at all, it's time to start keeping track of everything. This not only helps you track your profit but also helps you catch errors that may have occurred during transactions, at your bank, or in previous records. Beyond that, it's a necessary step to make sure you're following all of the applicable business rules, and it will help you make smarter decisions, too.

First, develop a filing system so you can save every receipt, invoice, and statement related to your venture. This doesn't have to be elaborate or complicated. A cardboard box with some paper folders is good enough. Break the income and expenses down into broad categories that make sense for your venture, such as advertising expenses, donations, sales, and operating expenses. Don't get too hung up on this right now—there is no one perfect method. Your venture will grow and change, and you can create new folders or reorganize things anytime you need to.

Second, set up a system to make a record of every time money comes into your accounts or goes out of them. Many business owners use QuickBooks Online, Kashoo.com, or Outright.com, which are computerized ledgers that automatically do the math to update your balances. An even easier (and cheaper!) way to keep track of your transactions is in a simple spreadsheet (like Microsoft Excel or Google Drive). You can also buy a preprinted paper ledger, or just make columns on a blank sheet of paper. If you do it yourself in a spreadsheet or on paper, set up the following columns and fill them in as in this example:

DATE	DESCRIPTION	VENDOR / CUSTOMER	AMOUNT $ (- FOR PAID, + FOR RECEIVED)	BALANCE
				$768
Jan. 15	200 Flyers	Vistaprint	- $25	$743
Jan. 22	Class tuition	Dance students	+ $200	$943

Whichever method you use, be sure to record your transactions as soon as possible, every time, so you don't forget anything.

BANKING

You may also want to think about opening a bank account. Some entrepreneurs start off using their own personal accounts or those of their parents or other adult mentor, and this is fine in the beginning. Eventually, though, you'll probably find it easier to open accounts specific to your venture. This way, you can track your income and expenses more easily and simplify your venture's record-keeping.

There are many different types of financial institutions to choose from, including banks and credit unions, and each has its own rules about how their accounts work. There are also different types of accounts available with many different options—ask each bank what it offers. A simple savings account may suit your needs perfectly. Or you might want to get a full-featured business checking account with a debit card, line of credit, online merchant services, accounting system integrations, detailed reports, and so on. Be wary of taking advantage of credit or loan offers, no matter how tempting they may be. It's far better if you can bootstrap your venture yourself, getting it started without relying on borrowing.

Check the minimum balance and other requirements. And always, always know what fees the bank might charge you. Don't be afraid to ask if there are other account options that might avoid the fees, especially for a young person. Some banks and credit unions have special accounts with lower fees and minimums just for students. There are several websites that can help you compare account options such as FindABetterBank.com, Money-Rates.com, or BankFox.com. Check several different institutions to see which one will give you the most favorable terms.

If you're under eighteen, you'll most likely need an adult to sign for the bank account with you, so ask a parent or your mentor to help you. You might want to have your treasurer or other members of your team on the account as well, so they can handle transactions without you present. Each of you will need to bring some identification (like your driver's license or birth certificate) and your social security number. And, of course, you'll need at least a small amount of money for the initial deposit.

Once you have your account set up, be sure to check the statements every month to make sure the bank's records match your own records. Accounting errors happen, and you'll want to catch them as soon as possible when they do!

TAXES

If you're making money, you will probably need to pay taxes—or at least file the right forms to prove that you don't need to pay them—even if you're under eighteen and just trying to help people. There are different kinds of taxes, but the ones you need to pay special attention to are income taxes and sales taxes. Income taxes are a percentage of your venture's income that must be paid to the federal government (and sometimes state and local governments, too). Sales taxes are a percentage of a product's purchase price paid by the buyer—and collected by the seller—which is then passed on to the government (usually state and sometimes county and city). The governments use tax money to pay for various programs like national security, education, roads, fire and police departments, and other programs that benefit the public.

Not every endeavor is big enough to warrant worrying about taxes. But if you're surprised by wild success, you may find yourself in that position. You pay income tax on money that you earn whether or not you have a business, but businesses get to deduct some of the money they spend—their expenses—from the amount they pay taxes on. If starting a business or nonprofit was an easy way to not pay taxes on the money that you earn, everyone would do it! To prevent people from abusing the system, the government has rules to determine whether a particular business expense is tax deductible or not. You don't want your venture to pay any more taxes than necessary, so you should claim the expenses that *are* deductible. To do that, you'll need to know—and be able to document—everything that is a legitimately deductible business expense.

It helps if your bookkeeping system keeps these different expenses in separate categories, so you can easily review them when the time comes to talk about income taxes. Here are some broad categories that most businesses find useful:

- Salaries and Benefits: If your organization pays anyone for work, even indirectly with benefits like free stuff, those payments fall under special tax rules for employers. Take good notes on these payments: where the money went, what it was for, and why it was necessary. There are a lot of gray areas: taking the whole team to a movie to celebrate a success could be a completely tax-deductible business expense, while giving a single employee a booklet of movie passes could be partially deductible—or not at all. Good notes about each expense will help your tax advisor help you untangle this when he's helping you file your venture's first tax return.

- Assets: Purchases of expensive equipment that will be useful for several years or more are treated differently than normal business expenses. Such purchases are treated as assets that can't all be deducted immediately. Instead, the deduction must be spread over several years. If you can avoid large purchases that trigger the rules (usually over $1000), that's simplest. But for the sake of the organization, you don't want to lose track of assets like this anyway, so starting an asset spreadsheet is smart. The sheet would track what the asset is, when it was purchased, for how much, and who has it now. Keep that up to date every time equipment is borrowed, moved, or retired.

- Meals and Entertainment: When is something that benefits your team not salary or benefits? When there's a clear business purpose for it. Unfortunately, like the movie example above, the rules can sometimes seem as clear as mud. So if you're treating your team or partners to food or fun, keep these expenses separate with better-than-usual notes about who, what, and why. If you have a for-profit business, some of these expenses may only be 50 percent deductible, some 100 percent, and some zero. Your good notes will help your tax advisor figure this out later.

- Clear business expenses: If you purchase an item or service because your venture needs it and only your venture will use it, then you have a clear business expense. Just keep the receipts (in electronic form, at least) and enter the transaction in your ledger. As long as you don't miss an expense entirely, you've got it covered.

1. Look over your venture's expenses to see if any of them might fall into any of the preceding broad categories.

2. Mark them accordingly. You might want to color code the expenses or just make a distinguishable mark in the margin.

3. Whatever your system, be sure to take good notes so you and others can understand the code easily.

4. Now that you have a system for marking these four categories, use it every time you enter a transaction in your venture's ledger.

Sales taxes are another issue. If you're the buyer in a transaction, you pay the taxes and you're done. But if you're the seller in a transaction, you need to charge the buyer the appropriate sales tax amount, keep track of all such transactions for a given period of time, and then pay the government periodically. The rules for sales tax vary by state and locality, so you'll have to see what rules apply to your venture.

In My Experience

When I was first considering launching a second career as a writer, I was actually more nervous about all the business stuff that would be involved than I was about the actual writing part. I'd been around entrepreneurs my whole life, and I'd successfully managed my personal finances for years, but somehow keeping track of my business budget, financial records, income and expenses, bank statements, taxes . . . oh my. It all sounded like so much work—and I had a college math degree! What scared me was thinking I'd have to learn a bunch of specific rules, master strange systems, and acquire new habits. Would I even have time to write with all of the necessary business management chores? And what if I made a mistake?

Despite my anxiety, I jumped in anyway. What I learned is that it's really easy. It doesn't take very much special knowledge or time at all. And the only habit I had to learn was to make a note on every receipt related to a business expense and drop it in a folder with the others. And mistakes? Well, I'm sure I've probably made a few along the way, but anyone who looks at my records will see that I do a pretty good job. The records are all in one place, they're straightforward and easy to interpret, and nothing jumps out as questionable. And that's pretty much all you need to do.

The writing part? Well, that took just a little bit longer to figure out.

LEARNING FROM THE NUMBERS

Money makes the world go around, so in your leadership role, you must familiarize yourself with the numbers. Now that you have your venture's books and bank accounts, check to see if you are spending money where your original business plan predicted. If not, do the differences make sense? Look for red flags and opportunities to improve, optimize, and revise the plan.

For example, if you discover the secretary has spent $50 on printing costs this month, when only $10 was allocated in the budget, you'll have to find a way to make up for that higher expense. Or, if you're selling a product, you may discover you've been selling at a loss after all the organizational costs have been accounted for. Either expenses must go down, or the price must go up.

If you're planning for next month or next year, you'll also have to keep an eagle eye on cash flow. It would be great to fly everyone to that event next summer, but given current income and expenses, will you have enough cash accumulated by then to afford it?

Many of these things are specific to your venture, so a standard bookkeeping system isn't enough. When you have a specific question or detail you need to investigate, think about creating a spreadsheet to analyze things in a tailored way. Online tools like Google Drive and Microsoft Office 365 let you share the load and work on those spreadsheets, in real time, with your advisors and others on your team.

Most of all, give yourself the time and tools to be able to go over the numbers frequently. Look at the data from different angles and perspectives. With time, you'll get good at understanding and managing the flow of money. You won't waste it or get caught short. And you'll put that cash to work for what your venture intended—having the best possible impact on the world.

YOUR MONEY MIND-SET

All of this might seem like overkill at first. After all, you're not a *Fortune* 500 CEO, right? But how you approach the financial stuff can make a big difference in your success or failure. "Even though Youth Ultimate Project is a youth venture with a small operating budget," Chris says,

"I learned that it is important for me to treat it with the same respect and seriousness that I would if I was working at any large corporation." If you don't set high goals and produce quality work, he says, how can you expect others to support and invest in you? Having a solid financial plan will set a strong foundation for success now and in the future.

Having been endowed with the gift I possess, I believe it is my duty to make money and still more money and to use the money I make for the good of my fellow man according to the dictates of my conscience.

John D. Rockefeller, industrialist and philanthropist,
in an interview with William Hoster, as quoted by
John T. Flynn in *God's Gold*

| 10 |
The Art of Making Money

It is not the creation of wealth that is wrong, but love of money for its own sake.

Margaret Thatcher, former Prime Minister of the
United Kingdom, in a speech to the General Assembly of the
Church of Scotland on May 21, 1988

As you learned in the budget portion of the previous chapter, you're going to need money to make things happen. You've already planned out your budget, so you know about how much you'll need, and you've done a little research on where it might come from. Here's where you really dig in to understand the various sources of income and start taking steps to make it all happen. Some of the ways you may be able to get money are asking for donations, applying for grants, and earning income through your own activities. This chapter will take a look at each of these potential sources of income. Be sure to have your venture journal handy so you can take notes about any ideas that pop up while you read!

In 2010, after an inspiring volunteer experience in an underprivileged village in Nicaragua, Daniel Martinez decided to create his own social venture when he arrived back home in Boston, Massachusetts. Three friends joined him. Together they represented cultures from Haiti, the Dominican Republic, Colombia, and the United States, so they decided to name the venture Les Manos United: a combination of three languages—French, Spanish, and English—which means "the united hands."

Because of their own diverse backgrounds, they decided to bring cultural awareness to high school students in their community and around the world in order to create more harmony and cooperation. They wanted to engage youth in discussions about world issues and then involve them in making a difference in those causes they felt passionate about.

Their first project, organized in 2010, was to send Christmas toys to children in Bas Gourmand, Haiti. It was quite successful, Daniel says. "I was surprised by the great amount of collaboration we got from people in school and the community, who donated toys and money and made it possible for us to complete our first project."

The following summer, the other three founders graduated, went to college, and left Les Manos United, but Daniel continued. He recruited new members from his high school to help, and they organized their second project around Daniel's upcoming service trip to Haiti and the Dominican Republic. This time, through their fundraising and supply drives, they were able to film a documentary about people's access to clean water in those countries. They also distributed shoes and sandals to people in the western Bateys in the Dominican Republic. In addition, they collected school supplies and books for schools in Matagalpa, Nicaragua, which they sent with other volunteers traveling there.

Back home, Daniel focused his efforts on using the documentary to raise awareness at his high school about issues affecting third world countries. In addition, Daniel traveled to Jinotega, Nicaragua, on a service learning trip, where he taught English and an environmental awareness workshop to children in primary school.

Daniel has been accepted into Harvard University; his tuition will be paid in full for four years by the Gates Millennium Scholarship, which he won as a result of his work with Les Manos United. "I am proud to have followed my passions and interests," Daniel says. "I aspire to continue my mission on a bigger scale in the future and create a nonprofit organization." He plans to keep solving real-life problems and hopes his projects will continue to make a difference in the lives of others and in his own.

DONATIONS

One way to raise money is to solicit donations from individuals, businesses, or both. When a product, service, facility, or other resource is donated directly, saving you the need to pay for it yourself, it's called an in-kind donation. These types of donations are often easier for businesses to make than cash. Analyze your budget and see if any of the items on your upcoming expenses list are things that might be offered by local businesses.

For example, maybe your budget includes printing flyers at an estimated cost of $180. Start by approaching a local print or copy shop and asking the manager if she would consider donating the cost of the printing. Offer to give the company credit for its support, such as printing a note at the bottom of the flyer acknowledging their donation. If she says no, ask if she'd be willing to at least offer you a discount. If you're a 501(c)(3) nonprofit, the business may offer a special rate. (See chapter 15 for more information on this official type of nonprofit organization.) Whether the company ends up helping you or not, always thank the manager for her time. Maybe next time you ask she'll be more willing to offer support.

Let's take a look at your business plan and see if we can take care of some of those expenses right now.

1. Look at the items listed in your expenses section. Could any of them be donated directly by businesses or individuals? Make a list with those items in the left-hand column.

2. Next to each item on your list, brainstorm who might be able to donate them to you.

3. Recruit volunteers from your team to contact those people or places and ask for the donations.

4. If you are able to procure any of your supplies this way, be sure to update your budget with "donated" instead of the cost, and reduce your necessary expenses accordingly!

Another way to collect in-kind donations is by setting up a donation bin. Sometimes you can persuade the management of a retail store to allow you to place a donation bin near the front entrance. If you're helping animals, for example, you might try setting up a bin, box, or barrel for pet food donations near the checkout line of a local grocery store. Design the container so shoppers know the name of your venture, what items you're collecting, and why—as well as how they can help. Then check in periodically to collect any donated items.

Donation bins can also be used to collect money instead of goods. You've probably seen the cans at the checkout lines asking for spare change. You can do the same thing by asking local stores and restaurants to let you place your own collection cans. Target those businesses that are related to your venture's activities: the shoe store, for example, if you're buying shoes for homeless children. Then decorate the cans with the necessary information and drop them off.

Of course, for some businesses and many individuals, it's easier to just give you cash or write a check—but you'll have to ask them to. You can do this by going door-to-door; standing outside a busy shopping area (ask the store manager first!); sending out emails, postcards, or letters; or by using a website like TheWorldWeWantFoundation.org, StartSomeGood.com, Piggybackr.com, Indiegogo.com, GoFundMe.com, or Kickstarter.com.

One special kind of donation is called a sponsorship. When a company sponsors your venture, you get the financial support you need in exchange for giving the company some good publicity on your website or printed materials, such as an event program. This can be a win-win situation, so it's worth approaching businesses to see if they'd be interested. For example, if you're running skateboarding camps for kids, you might ask your local sporting goods store if it would sponsor your venture if you agree to put its logo on the T-shirts you give to every camper. Just like with the donation bins, it's good to target businesses that are related in some way to your venture's mission.

No matter which donation-gathering method you decide to use, be ready once again to put your elevator pitch to work. Tell potential donors who you are, what you're doing, and why—then tell them how and why they should help. Be ready to make connections beyond donations! Have a way to collect contact information from people who are interested but unable to donate right then. It's also a good idea to have business cards that show your venture name, website address, and your contact information (email address or phone number). Don't worry if you don't have all of this set up yet, though. There's more information on promoting your venture in chapter 11.

Speaking of the website, when you make it, be sure to include information about how people can donate directly. Adding a Buy Now button to your site is an easy way to collect funds. Be careful though! Some states have laws prohibiting this without having the proper licenses on file, so make sure it's legal before you put it out there. Your adult mentor can help you look up the laws in your state.

Wherever you get your donations from, keep in touch with your donors—whether individuals or businesses—whenever possible. Thank them, invite them to events, and let them know how you're progressing. They earned it by contributing to your cause this time, and you'll also build relationships and keep them involved as potential sources of support in the future.

GRANTS

A grant is a special kind of donation, usually given by a government, charitable foundation, or company and distributed on a regular basis. Like a donation, a grant is free money given to you because someone wants to support your cause. But grants are different from other donations in a few important ways.

First, grants are usually large, starting at several hundred dollars and going up from there. Just one grant award could potentially cover all of your startup costs and get you off on the right foot with your operating expenses, whereas you would probably need to solicit many donations from individuals or businesses to receive that much. In order to achieve their goals, Les Manos United organized fundraisers, held supply drives, and applied for and won grants. In 2010 and 2011, they received $2,000 from the United Way to fund their venture. "Later, we obtained $2,500 from the ArtScience Prize to produce two documentary films concerning secondary education in Nicaragua and water access in communities in the Dominican Republic and Haiti," Daniel says.

However, grants can be harder to get than donations. You will have to research appropriate grant opportunities and prepare and submit a grant proposal—a formal document explaining why your venture deserves to be awarded the money—in order to get one. Luckily, most of what the grant makers want to know is already in your business plan, so you should already be ahead of the game there.

Also, every funder is a different organization operating under its own rules, so each has its own unique procedures for applying for its grant. Each grant application package you submit will require its own research and preparation time. It can be hard to know if preparing grant applications is the best use of your time or not, since you can never be sure you'll be awarded any grant you apply for.

Finally, because the grant makers are soliciting proposals from many different organizations like yours, evaluating them, and then making their decisions, actually receiving the grant can take a long time—and, in the end, you might not even be approved. So, if you're thinking about going for a grant, set aside a good deal of time to research funders, prepare the grant proposal, and wait for the money. You'll also need a backup plan in case that money never comes!

There are a few things you can do to increase your odds of receiving a grant, though:

- Do your research. Don't bother applying for a grant that you're not eligible for. You may need to be a resident of the city, county, or state in which the grant is being offered. You may need to be a registered 501(c)(3) nonprofit corporation. You may need to be over eighteen, or under twenty-four, or who knows! The grant makers are giving the money away, so they can make whatever rules they choose.

- Follow directions. Answer all of the funder's questions in the required format before the submission deadline.

- Show that you are already up and running, or at least are ready to be as soon as you receive the grant. This will help the funder feel more confident about giving you the money.

- In the proposal, lay out exactly what you will do with the money if you are selected.

- Show that you've thought about the future. Funders will be much more likely to invest in a venture that will continue for the long term, rather than one that is doing a one-time activity. Remember the long-term goals you wrote in your business plan, and see chapter 17 for more about sustainability.

- Form a partnership. This is, of course, optional, but if the grant makers see that multiple organizations are involved in the venture, they may feel like they're helping more people. See chapter 16 to learn about forming partnerships.

- Register as a 501(c)(3) nonprofit, or secure the fiscal sponsorship of one (see chapter 15). This is optional, but some funders only consider nonprofit organizations, so having this registration will open more opportunities for grants. It takes time and money to file this registration, though, so keep that in mind.

It you do win a grant, be sure to thank the funder. If you don't win a grant you applied for, don't be afraid to follow up with the funders and ask them why you weren't selected. They might give you valuable tips to help you improve your proposal for next time.

For more information about writing grant proposals, you can visit The Foundation Center's web page at foundationcenter.org.

Some organizations that can help you find grants specifically for youth-run social ventures are:

- DoSomething.org, dosomething.org/grants

- Youth Service America, ysa.org/grants

- The FreeChild Project, freechild.org/funds4progress.htm

Some other places to research grants include:

- Ashoka's Changemakers, changemakers.com/opportunities

- The Foundation Center, foundationcenter.org/findfunders

- The Grantsmanship Center, tgci.com/funding.shtml

- Grants.gov, grants.gov

But there are so many more! Check with your city, county, and state officials as well as citizen groups like Kiwanis, Rotary Club, Elks Club, and so on to see if there are any local sources of funding that might be available to you.

In addition to giving you money, grants can help you establish your venture in other ways. First, they add a bit of prestige and clout, because people will know that you had to submit a serious proposal and that your venture beat out other applicants. Also, you will probably get a fair bit of publicity, as the funders will publish the names of their grant winner(s) in their newsletters and on their websites. Newspapers and magazines might write about grant winners too! This will lead people to your venture whom you never could have connected with on your own. Finally, you may meet people from the funder's organization who can mentor or coach you in some way. These other benefits could, in the end, be more valuable than the money itself, so applying for grants can be well worth the effort.

MAKE YOUR OWN

Of course, you don't have to rely on the kindness of strangers (or friends and family) for funding. You're an entrepreneur, after all—you can make your own money! Earning your own income has some pretty big advantages: it puts you more in control of your budget, you don't have to convince people to give you something for nothing, and you get the personal experience of running a business—in addition to changing the world!

There are a three major ways to get people to pay you: you can sell a product, you can perform a service, or you can put on an event.

Selling a product could be something like making and selling the T-shirts we discussed earlier, holding a rummage sale, making jewelry and selling it at a farmer's market or on Etsy.com, or selling candy like Team Revolution did. Go back to chapters 3 and 4 and look at your passions, skills, and problems. Think about whether you can turn any of those into a salable product. Have a meeting with your team to brainstorm ideas based on everyone's passions, skills, and emotions. You might want to develop a new invention or idea, or go with something simple that you already know people want to buy. What do you see your friends, classmates, and neighbors buying? Is there a way for you to customize it and make it your own? Consider how much supplies will cost, how much time it will take to create the product, who might be interested in buying it, and how you will reach them. Then make it happen!

Services can be traditional things like mowing lawns, walking dogs, cleaning houses, or babysitting; or more modern ideas like designing web pages for people, teaching seniors how to use social media, or teaching younger students how to program software. If you can do something, you might be able to find someone who is willing to pay you to do it. You might engage in a group service, like a car wash, with your whole team. Or maybe each of you will go off and perform individual services that match each of your skill sets and interests, and then pool your earnings. Either way, you'll need to figure out how much your time is worth and how much customers typically pay for the service and then charge accordingly. Then get the word out so people know how to hire you and what you're raising the money for.

You could also raise money by hosting an event like a concert, a movie screening, a bouncy house, or a mini-carnival. Putting on an event can be fun and attract attention for your venture, but it also takes a lot of organization and time and can have big financial risks. You'd need to figure out what kind of event to have and where and when to host it. There are also the matters of how people will get there, how to tell them it's happening, how much staff the event will require, and how much each of those elements will cost, not to mention estimating how many people will come and how much you need to charge to make a profit.

Just because it's complicated doesn't mean you shouldn't do it, though! Just make sure you know what you're getting into first. Chapter 14 will cover details about event planning, so if you like this idea, make sure to keep reading!

In My Experience

While I'm all for raising money for social ventures, I'm personally not a fan of selling things. Whether I was a Girl Scout selling cookies or a teenager selling magazines, the word fundraiser *always made me cringe. Now that I have children of my own, it isn't any better—going door-to-door selling popcorn, candy, and poinsettias to our neighbors: yuck! If I had the money, I'd write a check for whatever amount we could make with the sale, just to avoid asking people to buy things. Most people don't mind supporting a good cause, but I still hate asking.*

I've come to really enjoy other kinds of fundraisers, though, both as an organizer and as an attendee. Charity events like auctions are enjoyable to attend and make big money for their causes. The conference I helped organize for SCBWI Western Washington was our biggest money-maker of the year. As an individual, I regularly attend several organizations' annual fundraising dinners. I get to enjoy a good meal with my friends, and the organizations get to tell me about their good deeds and ask for a check. Win-win!

Of course, other people love selling things. They're good at it. It energizes them. And that's just fine with me . . . especially if I can get them on my team so they can do the selling for me!

HYBRIDS

Finally, remember that there are many ways to combine these methods of raising funds. Perhaps you're worried that not everyone in your target audience can afford a ticket to the concert you're planning. It might work to ask for a suggested donation instead. Most people will probably pay up, others will see that it's a donation and give more than suggested, and those that can't afford to pay will still be able to attend.

Another option is to request money to support an activity that will make even more money. For example, you might collect donations or submit a grant proposal to cover the cost of having custom T-shirts printed. Then you can turn around and sell those T-shirts for more than you paid to make them, thereby keeping all of the revenue for your venture.

Just be honest with donors and funders about how you're going to spend their money and be transparent about the results, even if they're disappointing. Donors and funders will appreciate your efforts—and your honesty.

OTHER OPTIONS

You might be able to get investors to purchase shares of your venture. Doing so generally means you give up partial ownership of and control over your venture—plus a share of your future income—in exchange for their up-front capital. This is complicated, so it's best saved for later.

If all else fails, you may want to ask for a loan. Be careful, though! Depending on the interest rate and loan terms, you may end up paying back more money than you borrowed. And no matter what, loans need to be repaid, so only consider a loan if you're certain you can pay it back on time. Your adult mentor should be able to help you consider the pros and cons of taking out a loan or using other kinds of credit.

A PENNY SAVED...

No matter where your money comes from, make sure it goes as far as it can for your venture. It's time to get thrifty! Before buying something new, think about ways to get it used instead. Consider whether buying in bulk might make sense and save you money in the long term. And what about borrowing short-term or single-use items? You might be able to ask your mom if you can use her laptop and projector for your upcoming event, for example, rather than buying them yourself.

DOUBLING BACK

Now that you've thought more about all of your different fundraising options, it's a good time to go back to the goals and budget sections of your business plan and see how well your fundraising choices fit in. You may need to adjust your fundraising ideas to match your business plan, or perhaps you'll want to update your business plan to reflect your fundraising goals and their budget impacts. One way or the other—or even some of each—be sure to keep your actions in sync with your business plan. Each should continue to inform the other as your venture grows and evolves.

> It is the man who carefully advances step by step, with his mind
> becoming wider and wider ... persevering in what he knows
> to be practical, and concentrating his thought upon it, who is
> bound to succeed in the greatest degree.
>
> Alexander Graham Bell, inventor, scientist, and teacher, as quoted
> by Orison Swett Marden in *How They Succeeded*

| 11 |
How to Sell Well

Marketing is storytelling. . . . Your product and your service and your people are all part of the story. Tell it on purpose.

Seth Godin, author and entrepreneur, on his blog on October 4, 2012

Marketing refers to everything you'll use to promote your venture, its mission, and even its fundraisers! Marketing can include methods that cost money, like paying for advertisements, as well as free publicity tactics, like sending press releases to invite the media to write articles about your venture. Do you need to promote a specific product, service, or event? Or maybe you want to recruit more volunteers, solicit donations, or simply spread the word about your idea. A good marketing plan will include the strategies and tools you need to accomplish those goals.

Profile

BAKING FOR BREAST CANCER

Zach Steinfeld loves to bake. When he was middle school, he started experimenting with different recipes. By the time he entered high school at Pace Academy in

127

Atlanta, Georgia, he could make all kinds of brownies, cookies, muffins, cakes, cupcakes, and more. He made more than he and his family could eat themselves, so he often brought treats to school—which, as you can imagine, was a big hit!

When his dad suggested he put this love of baking to an even better use, Zach—then a sophomore—started the Baking for Breast Cancer Club with help from junior Jenna Blumenthal. Zach had several relatives who had been affected by breast cancer, so he and Jenna decided to donate their proceeds to the National Breast Cancer Foundation. Their very first bake sale earned $400.

At first, Zach's parents donated all the baking supplies and marketing materials, and all of the money raised at each bake sale went directly to the National Breast Cancer Foundation. This made the money management a little easier, but wasn't sustainable. "One of the most challenging parts of operating the club was handling the money," Zach says. "I had to find a balance between using the money donated by my parents and that raised by the sales themselves."

But Zach's organizational skills helped him find a way to balance the sales income, donations, and expenses. Being organized also helps him plan the sales, develop the schedule, and set up the tables at each sale. "One thing that separates our sales from other sales is our look," Zach explained. "I made sure that everything was lined up, that the pink signage was lined up and spaced evenly, that the pink tablecloth was laid out neatly, and that the donut boxes were preopened and easy to get to (the flavors were stacked separately, of course). People know our bake sales when they see them."

Just as important as the look of the table is the look of the marketing materials. "If no one knows about a bake sale in advance, then it is more than likely that they will either forget to bring money or neglect to find the bake sale. I didn't really understand this until after the first bake sale, which raised much less than I had hoped for," Zach says. "As the sales continued, though, I got the hang of advertising. My emails to the student body became much more polished, we started putting up posters, our tables became more visually appealing, and word of mouth increased exponentially." Almost every sale earned more than the one before it, and by the end of Baking for Breast Cancer's second year, everyone was saying that it had "monopolized" bake sales at the school.

It wasn't easy, but Zach says he has always been driven by his end goal of raising $12,500 and by the idea that he was helping people in need. "It has given me a higher purpose," he says, "and I feel accomplished and proud as a result."

WHAT IS MARKETING?

Let's look at the details that make up marketing. Businesses think about marketing as being made up of the five Ps:

- Product: whatever it is you're offering, whether it's a physical product, a service, or an event

- Price: how much you're asking people to pay for your product, even if it's free

- Place: where you will connect your product, service, or event to your customers

- Packaging: how you present your product in an appealing way and protect it, if necessary

- Promotion: the advertising and publicity you use to make people aware of your venture and its activities

You've probably already figured out your first three Ps through the exercises in previous chapters. Your packaging will most likely be pretty basic for now, and that's okay. The thing to focus on while you're getting the word out about your new venture is promotion!

BRANDING

For any kind of promotion, it's helpful to have an established and recognizable brand. A brand is the name, symbol, or design that distinguishes an organization from other, similar organizations. Zach demonstrates this with Baking for Breast Cancer's recognizable pink tablecloths, pink signage, and neatly displayed baked goods. Branding is more than just a trademark; it's the organization's overall public image. Three elements work together to create an organization's brand: its name, logo, and messaging.

Hopefully by now you have your name picked out (if not, there are some tips in chapter 8). The next thing you need is a logo to go with it. A logo is an image that represents an organization. A good logo is unique, accurately conveys your message, and fits with your venture's mission. It is simple, clear, and easy to read, so it looks good and is recognizable even if it's printed in black and white or is out of focus.

Take some time to brainstorm and sketch ideas for a logo in your venture journal, and ask your team for their thoughts, too.

Now that you have some good logo sketches, it's time to officially design your logo. Work closely with your technology guru and your public relations person to make a logo that best represents your venture. Some companies spend thousands of dollars on this, but for now, you can probably make one without hiring a professional graphic designer or buying expensive software. Try using free software like Inkscape to make designs based on your sketches. Or download free or inexpensive stock art from websites like sxc.hu or iStockphoto.com, and then use Inkscape to add your own design flair and make it unique for your company. Or, if no one on your team has the skills, tools, or time to create the logo, you could hold a logo design contest at your school or at one of your events.

You could also pay someone to design a logo for you using a low-cost web service like LogoDesignTeam.com or TheLogoCompany.net.

Once you have a logo, use it everywhere! You can put it on your physical promotional items like letterhead, business cards, flyers, print newsletters, T-shirts, pens, and so on, as well as on your digital promotional efforts like your website, blog, social media profiles, email signature, virtual newsletters, and videos.

Another part of branding is messaging, which is the story you tell about your venture and its mission. To come up with the basic messaging for your venture, go back and look at your elevator pitch and your business plan. You should be able to identify your venture's primary mission. That is the message you want to send across all of your branding efforts.

No matter what form you use to deliver your message or whom you deliver it to—whether it's a video shown to other teen activists or a letter to potential donors—make sure your messaging is consistent. For example, don't tell pet owners that your venture's main goal is to help them keep their pets even if they can't afford to care for them, and then tell veterinarians that your venture's main goal is to offer low-cost spay and neuter surgeries. Of course, you will present your messaging a bit differently to different audiences, but the basic story you tell should always be the same. In the previous example, you could instead tell both audiences that your venture's main goal is to reduce the number of unwanted pets that end up in shelters.

Remember that your messaging is important for more than just your written materials. Every time you get the chance to say your elevator pitch, you're sharing your venture's story and raising awareness. Do it often, and do it well. The more you get your message out there—in any form—the more people will hear it, remember it, and support it.

PROMOTION TACTICS

Now that you've settled on your branding, it's time to put it to work! If you haven't established a web presence yet, now is the time to do so. Even if you're not ready to launch any substantial online campaigns yet, put up a basic website of some kind. You can make a webpage by setting it up yourself via a blog service like Blogger or WordPress, using a company like AcornHost.com to host web pages you design, or by using a full-service website marketing company like Web.com. If you want to have your own domain name, you can register one by going to a registration site like Name.com or Namecheap.com. This is fast and doesn't cost very much, so even if you don't need it just yet, it's probably worth doing it right away to reserve it until you're ready.

Setting up a website or blog can be a cheap, easy way to promote your venture online. Use your branding—name, logo, and messaging—to let people know about your venture. And, make sure you have some kind of contact information up there, so people can reach you if they have questions. Social media is an important part of virtual promotion, too, but we'll talk more about that in the next chapter.

The internet makes promotion easy, but sometimes physical items are best. One of the most important of these is business cards. You can design them on your own computer and then print them on specially made cardstock or order them online from a website like Vistaprint.com or us.moo.com. Business cards don't cost much, so hand them out every chance you get.

You might want to put up flyers or posters to promote your venture or one of its upcoming events. Maybe your school will even let you take over a bulletin board to showcase your venture's activities or set up an information table during lunch or other school functions. Baking for Breast Cancer, for example, really gained momentum after Zach and his team started hanging posters around the school to make students aware of upcoming sales. Also, if you're selling something, consider printing coupons or gift certificates to entice people to buy while getting your name and logo out there. "One thing I wish someone had told me," Zach says, "is that people respond very positively to incentives!"

Print postcards and mail them to supporters, prominent members of the community, and reporters. Put the same information on a handbill (a smaller flyer) and hand them out to people walking by at school or in town. You could look into getting items like T-shirts, pens, or bracelets with your logo on them to give away at events or to use as rewards for your key volunteers. CafePress.com can help you design and print custom items.

Some promotional activities can be both physical and digital! Photos of your venture's activities can liven up printed materials or those distributed via the internet. You can post images of your paper flyers and brochures online as well. Testimonials, which are quotes from people who have worked with your venture, are useful anywhere. Write a newsletter informing readers about what your venture has been up to and post it on your website, email it to supporters, and print and send it by regular mail to key partners. And if you buy classified ads for announcements about upcoming events or requests for volunteers, they now appear both in printed formats and online.

ADVERTISING

Many people think marketing and advertising are the same thing, but as you saw in the five Ps, advertising is really just a part of marketing. Still, it is a key part.

While all the free or inexpensive promotion tactics we just explored are great, sometimes the quickest way to promote something to a lot of people is to advertise it. Advertising is when one organization pays another for the purpose of calling attention to itself or its products. Advertising is all around you—television, radio, newspapers, Google, Facebook, YouTube . . . Sometimes it's obvious and in your face, while other times it's more subtle or even deceptive.

Remember, advertising costs money, so do everything you can to make sure it's effective. Successful advertising follows some basic principles for connecting with an audience: tell a story, make the audience feel something, and then tell them what you need from them. To do that, you need to understand your audience and address the question nearly every ad viewer asks: what's in it for me?

For every ad campaign you create, first ask yourself some key questions:

- Who is your primary target audience? For example, are you advertising to young people like yourself or to wealthy donors? Obviously, the way you present your message to each group will be different.

- How will you reach the most members of that target audience? What do they watch, read, and do? Where do they spend their time? How will your message find them? If you're advertising to wealthy donors, you might have better luck advertising in your local newspaper than on YouTube, for example. The best advertising message in the world doesn't do any good if the right people never hear it.

- What do you most want to communicate to that audience at this time? Is it a general campaign to raise community awareness about a problem, or is it a specific invitation to your next fundraising event? Advertising your upcoming event without telling people when it is and how to purchase tickets probably won't do you any good, so make sure you include key information. Thinking about your most pressing goals will help you focus your message.

- How will you know if your campaign reached that audience? Will you collect RSVPs, see retweets on Twitter, or wait for donations to pour in? Advertising costs money, so you'll want to be able to measure your success to know if you should do the next campaign the same way or try a different approach.

Many places that run ads, such as magazines and websites, have special requirements for submitting ads to them. These could include dimensions (sometimes measured in inches or sometimes in pixels), resolution (generally online ads are low resolution and print ads are high resolution), and how many words you can use in the space. Be sure to read and follow the requirements carefully so you don't have any problems getting your message out to your audience.

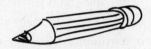

In My Experience

Like so many things in business, the best marketing tactic for someone else's venture may not be the best one for your venture. My husband's electronics company, for example, thrives on paid online advertising. My father's forestry business, though, was best marketed by word of mouth, as was my brother's tool and die shop. SCBWI Western Washington needed to use a number of marketing tactics, from websites to direct email campaigns to print materials. And my career as an author is currently best served by social media, although that will probably change.

The point is that every organization I've seen or been involved with has had its own unique approach to marketing, and that's just as it should be, since every business is unique. The only way to know what's going to work for you is to try something and measure your results. Then try something else and measure those results. Which one worked better? That's the path to follow—at least for now.

Keep trying different strategies and checking your results. Hmmm . . . come to think of it, maybe I'd better go design some custom bookmarks.

MAKING YOUR OWN MARKETING CAMPAIGN

From business cards to advertisements, there are endless possibilities to promote your venture. We can't forget social media! You're probably already talking up your new venture on the Twittersphere. And then there's traditional media, too. You can even try to get an article about your venture in a newspaper or magazine—in print or online. Both forms of media are great promotion, but they require a specialized approach. We'll talk more about working with the media in the next chapter.

All of these promotional suggestions are only meant to spark your own great imagination. Brainstorm in your venture journal and with your team, and you'll surely come up with unique and effective ideas. You don't have to do them all at once, though! Just be aware of the many opportunities for promotion, and do whatever feels the most natural at the time. Then evaluate how well it worked and let that guide your decision the next time you're looking to promote. Different methods will work better or worse depending on a variety of factors, and you'll soon discover which marketing niches are the most effective for you.

Without promotion, something terrible happens ... Nothing!

Often attributed to P. T. Barnum, founder of the
Ringling Bros. and Barnum & Bailey Circus

12

Working the Media

Whoever controls the media controls the mind.

Often attributed to Jim Morrison,
songwriter and lead singer for The Doors

A nother way to promote your venture is to make yourself available to the media and try to get news outlets and special interest organizations to feature your story. This can have many of the same benefits of advertising, but you don't need to pay anything for media coverage! You will need to put some time and energy into crafting your message and reaching out, though. This chapter will show you how.

Profile
STUDENTRND

Edward Jiang was on the robotics team at Interlake High School in Bellevue, Washington—one of the top public high schools in the country—but he was frustrated. He loved the communities surrounding the robotics competitions, but he felt like the competitions encouraged students to win awards just to list them on their resumés rather than to do something meaningful. He really wanted the time and resources to just play with technology alongside other enthusiasts and see what they could make out of it. So, right as he was about to graduate, he recruited some of his friends to spend the summer of 2009 hanging out with him at his house and building cool technology projects together.

As time went on, they realized they wanted to build a permanent place in the community where any student could do the same kinds of things they were doing. StudentRND was born. By 2013, StudentRND occupied a 3,500-square-foot office space in Bellevue, Washington. The location has an electronics lab (with soldering tools and oscilloscopes), a fabrication lab (with a 3-D printer and laser cutter), a computer lab (loaded with software packages), and an impressive technology library. StudentRND is now a registered nonprofit, and Edward and his team control a five-figure annual budget and receive more than a third of their funding from technology companies like eBay, Splunk, Coinstar, Stratos, and Medtronic.

One of the keys to their success, Edward says, is student-to-student marketing. "You have to start with those most passionate about your service, and then let it trickle down to other populations by word of mouth." And trickle down it has. StudentRND is rolling out its successful CodeDay program across the country, and in 2012, it launched a plan to double the number of students who participate in the summer program every year for three years, aiming for 240 students by 2015. Some of the students who designed or built projects at StudentRND have even used those projects to launch successful businesses of their own.

In addition to word of mouth, StudentRND's smart use of media has helped the group grow. If you search for StudentRND online, you'll see it's everywhere. The organization maintains a professional-looking web page as well as an active blog, Twitter feed, and Facebook page. How did the StudentRND leaders find student volunteers to organize CodeDays in cities across the country? They put it on their blog. How did they promote their upcoming technology showcase? They posted it on Twitter and Facebook, and got it on calendars at all of the local newspapers. StudentRND has even been featured in major online media outlets like

TechCrunch, *GeekWire*, and *Mashable*, as well as in traditional media like newspapers, radio, and television.

Still, Edward doesn't let that go to his head. For him, the best part of all the publicity is that StudentRND is reaching more students, engaging them in technology, and making real products. And that's what he wanted from the start.

SOCIAL MEDIA

The easiest way to showcase your message in the media is to do the sharing yourself! Social media puts you in charge, and using social media—like YouTube, Twitter, Facebook, Instagram, Vine, Tumblr, Reddit, Pinterest, and more—can be the quickest, cheapest, and easiest way to promote your venture. Plus, since most of us live online these days, it can also be very effective. This is great news! Here are a few tips to help you make the most of it.

First, accept that you can't be everywhere at the same time. There are too many social media platforms out there—and new ones popping up every day—for you to possibly hit them all. Each of them has its own culture, too, so you need some experience  before you can jump in and use them effectively. If you're already using a social network (or two or three), start there! Have your team members use the ones they're already using comfortably, too.

If you have time to explore other networks, feel free, but it takes a while to build a following on any new platform. After you've explored several, decide which ones feel like the best fit for you. Consider things like how easy they are for you to use, as well as what kind of audience each platform caters to—and what kind of audience your message needs to reach. Then, focus your efforts on just one or two of the best platforms for you and your venture. Also, be aware that there may be widgets and tools available that can help you hit several platforms at once, such as one that automatically sends an update to Twitter and Facebook whenever you post something on your venture's Tumblr page.

Next, make your message as interesting as possible by using photos, questions, anecdotes, and testimonials. As with your other promotional materials, use messaging that includes a story with structure, emotion, and relatability. Perhaps most important, don't be afraid to ask people to forward your message on to their own networks!

For example, while I'm writing this, I'm looking at StudentRND's Twitter profile. First, it features the logo and a picture of a teenager holding a laptop—with a StudentRND sticker on the lid! It has a tagline: "We're fixing tech ed and creating the next generation of technologists." It has a call to action—"Help us expand CodeDay to your city: codeday.org/organize"—along with its regular web address. And that's just in the profile! StudentRND marketers are also tweeting links to other places they've been featured in the media, talking about their most recent event, and retweeting people who mention them. They, in turn, are being retweeted by their followers, so their message is being spread to those who are most interested in hearing it with little effort or investment on their part.

In My Experience

I try to keep up with what's happening in social media. With my background in software engineering, the technology doesn't frighten me and I like to know what's out there. I have some level of presence on most of the major platforms out there today including Facebook, LinkedIn, Pinterest, Google+, YouTube, and Tumblr. I also have a website and a blog. My favorite online pastime, though—at least right now—is Twitter, so that's where I spend most of my time.

It's important for authors to have a platform—a dedicated group of fans who are interested in reading what we write. Over the last few years, I've gotten to where I have a decent number of followers, but I'm still growing my platform. It's largely unintentional, though. That is to say, I'm being honest and not just going after numbers. I never went out and asked people to follow me (although there's no reason why you couldn't). I never had any contests or giveaways (but I'm not saying that your venture shouldn't!). I just followed people I was interested in hearing more from, and I posted things I thought were interesting. I'm there to connect with like-minded people and organizations. I have fun.

That doesn't mean I sit back and relax and let Twitter promote my books for me, though. I have my own marketing plan, and I include social media as well as print, radio, and television. The more different audiences I can reach to tell them about my books, the better.

The thing to remember about social media is that although it's fun, it usually takes a long time to build your audience, and even then you can't reach everyone. It may be tempting and convenient, but don't focus all of your marketing energy there and think you've got it covered. Find other ways to reach out, even if they're more difficult, because you'll reach far more people in the long run—and they might end up following you on your favorite social media account, too.

TRADITIONAL MEDIA

It may seem like social media is all you need, but obviously, not everyone is going to be on the platforms you end up using. Don't ignore traditional media outlets like newspapers, magazines, radio, and television if you want to reach even bigger, more diverse audiences. Traditional media can still give your venture a huge boost, like it did for StudentRND.

Perhaps surprisingly, Edward says StudentRND doesn't have an official media strategy, but he and his colleagues do contact the press. "Whenever we do something newsworthy (a team of students build a cool project, for example), we try to tell reporters about it," he says. "Reporters are always looking for stories, so if you send them a message about something truly interesting, they're always excited to learn more about it."

The key is to attract reporters' attention, and the main way to do that is by distributing a great press release. What's a press release? It's really just a document announcing something newsworthy in a specific format that reporters are used to reading. That format looks like this:

- Headline: The title of your news story. Make it catchy but concise, using present tense and active verbs.

- Dateline: The city and state where your story takes place, with the date, at the beginning of the first paragraph.

- Lead: All of the most important facts in your story (the five Ws: who, what, where, when, and why) in three to five engaging sentences in the first paragraph. This might be as far as they'll read, so make sure to put the best stuff up front!

- Body: Additional paragraphs expanding on the facts in the lead paragraph. Give them ideas for how they can present the story.

- Quotes: These can be used in the body paragraphs to personalize the story or validate your claims.

- Boilerplate: The last paragraph, summarizing your venture and what you do in one to three sentences.

- Contact information: Who can they contact for more information, and how can they reach him or her?

- ###: This symbol means "The End." Place it in the center of the line right below your contact info.

Here's a hypothetical press release similar to what StudentRND might use to announce one of its events.

FOR IMMEDIATE RELEASE

StudentRND Announces Labs Demo Day

(Bellevue, Wash.) June 19, 2015—Come see what the 2015 class of StudentRND Labs has developed this summer!

Local student participants will demonstrate their innovative technology projects to the Seattle community on August 22, 2015, at the Ammi-Joan Paquette Room in the Seattle City Hall. Opening ceremonies will begin at 1:00 PM. Labs presentations will begin at 1:30 PM. Open demonstrations will run from 3:00 to 5:00 PM.

More than forty enthusiastic students spent eight weeks of their summer vacation at StudentRND Labs building amazing hardware and software with the latest technologies. On Demo Day, they will unveil their impressive projects to the general public for the first time. Tickets cost $10 per person and may be purchased in advance through Eventbrite or at the door.

"Demo Day was an incredible event last year!" said StudentRND's CEO Edward Jiang. "This year should once again be an exciting chance to meet some of the Seattle area's brightest young technology makers."

About StudentRND:
StudentRND is a registered 501(c)(3) nonprofit organization that runs programs to create the next generation of technologists. StudentRND Labs is its eight-week intensive summer program. The group also runs CodeDay, a nationwide network of 24-hour programming marathons for high school and college students.

```
Contact:     Edward Jiang
             CEO, StudentRND
Phone:       555-555-1212
Email:       ceo@studentrnd.org
Web page:    studentrnd.org


             # # #
```

Here are a few more things to keep in mind when writing your press release:

- It shouldn't sound like an advertisement. Make it read like a news story. What would make it interesting and relevant to readers, listeners, or viewers?

- Write it about you, not from you (use third person, don't use "I" or "we" except in the quotes).

- Tie it to a specific point in time like an award, an event, a new partnership, or a milestone.

- Reporters move quickly, but they still need time to write the story! Try to send your release four to six weeks before an event will take place.

- Make sure that someone who knows nothing about you or your venture can understand everything in the press release.

- Keep it single-spaced and left justified.

- It MUST be short enough to fit on one page!

WHERE TO SEND IT

It's tempting to go after major media coverage like the *Today* show or the Disney channel first, but those places receive thousands of press releases, so your efforts are probably better spent going after more local coverage, at least to start. Local news reporters are actively looking for stories from or about the communities they serve, so they are more likely to publish or broadcast your story. And that can be your ticket in, since larger media outlets look at what the smaller ones are covering. Even a short piece in a small, local newspaper can be seen and picked up by national media. So start small and build momentum over time.

Let's make a list of places where you could send your press release.

1. In your venture journal, build a list of all of the organizations you think may be interested in reporting your news story. Start by looking up your local newspapers, magazines, radio stations, and television stations. Ask people in your target audience what they read, listen to, and watch. You can also go to the library and look in reference materials like *The Standard Periodical Directory* (Oxbridge Communications) or the *Gale Directory of Publications and Broadcast Media* (Gale Research). Both of these directories list media outlets in the United States by state. The reference librarian can help you track down these and other resources.

2. Be sure to include the organizations' contact information. Be on the lookout for email addresses for specific reporters, or at least the address where they want general news story ideas to be sent.

3. Once you have compiled your list, try to rank the organizations according to which ones are the best fit, both for your promotional needs and for their news coverage needs. Send your press release to

your top five to ten choices. Sending it to too many might get you flagged as a spammer, and it will be awkward if too many say yes at the same time. If you don't get any responses within a week, move down the list to your next group of choices.

THE PRESS KIT

A press kit is simply a collection of basic information about your venture that can bring someone quickly up to speed. Having one makes it easier for people to report about you—and therefore more likely that they will—and also saves you from spending time answering their questions. Make it available in folders at events and as a downloadable PDF on your website. Here are some things you might want to include in your press kit:

- A letter introducing your venture and explaining why people should care about what you're doing

- Brief bios of you and your key team members

- Copies of recent press coverage you've received

- Copies of your recent press releases

- Photos

- Your venture's official logo

- A quick-reference fact sheet about your venture and the problem it is addressing

- A list of your venture's awards, grants, sponsors, partnerships, and so on

- A calendar of upcoming events

- Contact information for your venture in case someone wants to find out more

As you can see, you'll need to keep your press kit updated as your venture grows and changes, but it will save you time in the long run because it's a great way for people to find out more about your venture without contacting you directly.

OTHER MEDIA CONSIDERATIONS

There are a few other things to think about when it comes to media promotion. First, let everyone involved know ahead of time that you're seeking media coverage. Your school may have special requirements related to media interaction such as privacy protections and permission forms, so if your venture is at all school related, communicate with school officials about your plans before it's too late.

Second, after you send out a press release or launch a social media campaign, be ready for people to contact you! Practice your messaging and elevator pitch over and over again. Prepare some brief sound bites and relevant statistics that you can quote from memory. Be ready to share the limelight with your team, volunteers, allies, sponsors, and partners. Be flexible and help  reporters get the story they need, but don't waver from your values and mission. Relax and remember reporters are people too, just like you.

Third, be patient and don't expect quick results. "Many students think that getting in the news is the be-all and end-all to being successful, but usually there are few short-term benefits," Edward cautions. "I can't think of specific opportunities we've received because of media coverage, but it helps us build a brand as an organization that is actively changing the world, and it changes our external perception over time."

Finally, don't get so focused on your media strategy that you forget your goals and mission. Even though it's worked well for StudentRND, Edward advises against wasting too much time chasing after media. "It's nice to get an article or two so your team can feel good, and it's tempting to use it to build your college application or resumé," he says, "but I'd focus the majority of your time on actually building your organization and doing its activities. That'll pay off even more in the long run."

Young people around the world must reach out to help others realize their talents and make their voices heard.

Michelle Obama, First Lady of the United States of America, in a speech at Youth Forum in Mexico City on April 14, 2010

13

Speeches that Sparkle

We must get the American public to look past the glitter,
beyond the showmanship, to the reality, the hard substance
of things. And we'll do it . . . not so much with speeches that
will bring people to their feet as with speeches that bring
people to their senses.

Mario Cuomo, former governor of New York, in the Democratic
National Convention keynote address on July 16, 1984

Sooner or later, you'll get the opportunity to talk to other people
about your venture. Maybe you'll be doing some informal networking at a street fair. Or, perhaps you'll pitch your venture idea to people
who can help you. You might even be asked to deliver a speech to a
large audience at a formal event! For some people, this is a frightening thought. For others, it's exhilarating. However you feel about it,
there are ways you can make your public speaking experiences more
successful, and you'll need to know how to make the most of these special occasions when they arise. As Chris Trinh says, "I've learned how
to step out of my comfort zone and promote Youth Ultimate Project's
mission in the community . . . every single person I encounter can be a
potential supporter."

TRIPLE H (HOMELESSNESS, HUNGER, HOPE), GIRLS INC.

 Seventeen-year-old Rouaa Ahmad and eighteen-year-old Sucelyn Pojoy of Lynn, Massachusetts, didn't have to look very far to identify the problem they wanted to solve. "The inspiration for our idea," they say, "was seeing the homeless people in our neighborhoods and watching them go from trash bin to trash bin looking for food." The two young women decided to educate their community about the issues of hunger and homelessness while also raising money for a local hunger organization, My Brother's Table. "Not a lot of people realize that there are people in our community who have died from hunger or lack of shelter," Rouaa says.

With the help of their Girls Inc. advisor and their Ashoka Youth Venture mentors, the girls formed Triple H (Homelessness, Hunger, Hope) and came up with a multipronged plan: to raise money for My Brother's Table through sales of wristbands and cookbooks, and to organize a Faces of the Homeless panel event during National Hunger and Homelessness Awareness Week in November 2013. Once they had their plans in place, they presented to a Youth Venture selection panel in hopes of receiving a grant to cover their initial costs.

"I felt really nervous," Rouaa says. "It has always been tough for me to present or speak in front of other people." The members of Triple H knew that getting their presentation right would take a lot of advance preparation, so they started about a week early. They wrote their proposal, created a PowerPoint presentation, and divided the speech into parts. "Each member had to practice and rehearse their parts in front of our group advisor and mentors," Rouaa says. "Then, we thought ahead of some questions that the panelists might ask during the presentation and how we would be able to provide the information and answer these questions clearly."

On the day of the presentation, they arrived early, dressed professionally, and rehearsed one more time as a group. "It was a success, because we got funded to run our venture," Rouaa says. She remembers that even though she had a shaky voice from nerves, the audience was too focused on what she was saying to notice. And the panelists asked some of the questions Sucelyn and Rouaa had anticipated, so they had the answers ready to go.

"The more you practice," says Rouaa, "the better your presentation will be." That practice will also make you appear more confident when you're presenting. "Confidence will make a difference," Rouaa says, "because even if you mess up a little bit, people are not going to know as long as you show confidence and persistence."

During their first year, Triple H raised $300 through bake sales and wristband sales. The cookbooks turned out to be more difficult and time-consuming than Rouaa and Sucelyn planned, but they continued to work on them. And they were still planning to host the Faces of the Homeless panel.

"I feel like our venture has been a success because we got involved with events in the community, helped educate the public about the issue of homelessness, and raised money to fight hunger," Rouaa says. "However, this might be just the beginning of our great success."

FIRST IMPRESSIONS

As the saying goes, you never get a second chance to make a first impression. Whether you're having a casual one-on-one conversation or speaking in front of an audience, making a bad first impression could haunt you for a long time, no matter how many great things you do later. But a good first impression can make people more inclined to forgive later mistakes. Clearly, there's a lot riding on it. Fortunately, there are some easy ways to make your best possible first impression.

First, be on time! This one should be the easiest, but too many people don't take it seriously enough. Being late, even just a little, tells people that you don't care or aren't serious. And don't think you can get away with blaming it on traffic or other lame excuses. The best way to make sure you're always on time is to plan to arrive early for everything. Then, you'll be ready for all of the surprise delays, and they won't ruin your plans or make you look bad.

Next, you've probably heard that appearances don't matter, beauty is only skin deep, and you can't judge a book by a cover. This is all true ... mostly. When it comes down to it, obviously character is far more important than looks. But people will start forming opinions about you as soon as they see you, before they've had a chance to get to know you at all, so consider that when you're getting ready for a meeting or appearance. You don't have to be stunningly beautiful or ruggedly handsome, but you do need to look both respectful and respectable. It's okay to express your individuality, but find ways that won't clash with the expected fashions for the event. If your audience is going to have a negative reaction to your nose ring, for example, remove it for this particular event. People will respect you more if you show some respect for their social norms. And everything, including YOU, should be clean and neat. If ever you want to shower, put on deodorant, and brush your teeth, this is the time. Again, it shows you care about the people around you and that you respect yourself. And it'll go a long way toward making others respect you, too.

Another thing people notice very quickly is your body language. Even if you're nervous, standing tall but relaxed will make you appear both confident and competent. Keep your head up and look people in the eyes. Try not to fidget, bounce, crack your knuckles, check your phone, or do anything else that is repetitive or makes it seem like you're not paying attention. And be prepared to shake a lot of hands—firmly! If someone offers you their hand, don't be afraid to reach out and grab it.

If you're meeting someone new and there's no one to introduce you (or they forget), just introduce yourself—the sooner the better! And if you know other people in the crowd, do the introducing for them. They'll appreciate your thoughtfulness. Use people's names every chance you get (within reason, of course). It will help you remember them later, shows that you're interested in them, and makes the conversation feel more personal.

Be sure to listen to others at least as much as—or more than—you talk about yourself. Ask questions to draw them out, and nod your head occasionally to show you're paying attention and encourage them to elaborate. Most people love talking about themselves once they know what to say, so give them an opening, and then let them run with it. You can ask them what drew them to the event you're attending, what they're working on, and why. See if they have any advice for a young person like you. Ask about personal details, too. Find out about their hometowns, their family, their pets, their favorite sports teams, good books they've read lately, whatever! If it's something you care about also, you'll find common ground soon enough and have plenty to talk about.

If you're thinking all of this just sounds like common courtesy, you're right. Simply being polite is a huge asset. But your biggest asset is your smile. Seriously. Happy people are more fun to be around, so people will be more interested in getting to know you if you're smiling. They'll most likely smile back, too. You look more confident when you smile, and, believe it or not, smiling actually makes you *feel* more relaxed. So, just take a deep breath . . . and smile!

GOLDEN OPPORTUNITIES

There will be times when you need to do more than look decent and shake hands, though. Maybe you'll be reporting to your board of advisors about your venture's progress. Perhaps you need to appear before the city council to ask them for a change in policy. Imagine being interviewed on camera by your local television news anchor! At some point, you'll be asked to speak about your venture in front of people who can help you advance your mission. These are wonderful opportunities to spread the word about your venture—and get some of the recognition you and your team deserve!

Speaking in public can be scary for some people, of course. "A few days before my group did our PowerPoint presentation," Rouaa confesses, "I spent my whole time thinking about presenting in front of people that I would be meeting for the first time and about how I'm going to make my first impression on them through public speaking." But it really doesn't have to be that bad. Rouaa's advice? "Prepare ahead of time!" The biggest key to success is simply to be prepared. If you go in knowing what you are going to say and how you're going to say it, you'll not only be successful but enjoy yourself too. And the more you do it, the easier it will get. Let's look a little closer at some tips.

In My Experience

I used to be terrified of speaking in public. I once gave a speech to a room full of fellow employees at my company. After it was over, people told me I did well, but I had no recollection of anything from the time I stood up until I sat back down again! Fortunately, I've since come to enjoy giving presentations. I still get nervous, of course, but now it's more of a good energy than an "I'm going to die" panic.

When you sense that panicky feeling, it's all because of stress. Stress is your body's response to something threatening. It's supposed to wake you up, get you ready, so you can face the challenge before you—or run away from it. It's called the flight-or-flight response, and it's great if you're being chased by something that wants to eat you. But sometimes that stress can get in the way of doing what you want to do. A bad case of nerves can raise your heart rate to an uncomfortable level and leave you speechless.

How do I keep my stage fright from getting in the way? One thing that helps me now is to focus on the benefits of stress rather than trying to overcome it. When I'm getting ready to speak to a crowd, I take a moment to notice how I'm feeling. Wow, am I scared! Then I remember that all of that stress can help me do a better job. I'll be more energetic on stage. I'll think more quickly. I thank my body for stepping up and giving me this extra boost so I can be successful. This takes the edge off for me, and helps me focus on the task at hand—delivering my message to the audience.

A friend of mine takes a similar approach. He also pauses to notice how his nerves are making him feel. Then he gives himself time to just feel it—Wow, am I scared!—without trying to control it or make it go away. He acknowledges the fear and lets it fill him up for a few seconds. Then he can calm down and proceed with his talk.

You might have to experiment to find a technique that works for you. That's one of the reasons that you get better at speaking in public the more often you do it. Believe or not, even if you're scared of public speaking, you can become comfortable being in front of an audience, just like I have. All it takes is practice.

WHAT TO SAY

A speech is really nothing more than a story. Think about the last good book you read, or news story that affected you, or even something a friend told you that stuck with you. They're all stories, and your presentation should be, too.

All good stories share some basic characteristics. The best ones usually appeal to our logical brains as well as to our emotional cores. To do this, they need to have a well-organized structure and a lasting emotional resonance.

Structure just means the story has a clear beginning, middle, and end. Everything must fit together in a logical order. To develop your structure, think about where your audience is starting from and what knowledge they have about your mission already. Then, think about where you want them to be at the end of your talk. Your job is to deliver a speech that will first hook them so they want to hear more, and then connect all of the dots necessary to get them from their beginning point to your end point. If you don't have a solid structure, you'll lose some of your listeners along the way, so think of how each of your points connects to the next, and the next, and so on. Make sure they relate to each other so your story remains coherent throughout. Even if you know the audience could figure out how you got from one step to the next, don't make them do that work. Let them relax while you competently show them the way. The audience should feel like they've embarked on a journey with you as their expert guide. They may not know where they're going to end up, but each step should seem so effortless—without requiring them to make any big leaps—that they're perfectly willing to follow you. This doesn't mean that you need to be boring or predictable. Quite the opposite, in fact, as surprises can help keep people engaged in a story! But there's a big difference between being surprised and being confused.

No matter how well written a story is, if people can't relate to it personally they won't want to keep listening. That is where emotional resonance comes in. You need to make your speech—your story—appeal to your audience. "I've learned that as a public speaker, it is important to know exactly what my audience values and then cater my message to that specific audience in order to make a connection," says Chris from Youth Ultimate Project. "For example, my presentation to a major funder would be different from one to a group of high school students, because both audiences value different things."

The mistake most people make when giving a presentation is to focus on what makes their story emotionally relevant for themselves. Instead, think about it from the perspectives of your audience members. What does your story have to do with them? You're probably trying to get them to take some kind of action as a result of hearing your talk. What would make them do that? It might be the same reason you would do it, but it might not. At some level, nearly all listeners are asking, "What's in it for me?" If you can subtly answer that for them, you'll have a much better chance of getting them to do what you want.

Lastly, make use of rhetorical devices like repetition, alliteration, similes and metaphors, and irony. Use anecdotes and statistics. These will entertain your listeners and help keep them engaged in what you're saying.

Let's draft a potential speech in your venture journal.

1. First, think of a strong hook to use in the beginning. It might be a question that makes your audience reflect. It could be a shocking statistic about the problem your venture is tackling. It might be your personal story about how you became interested in your issue. Write down one good opening sentence.

2. You might think the middle comes next, but I like to write the ending before I write the middle. It helps me to know where I'm trying to go! Think about where you want your audience to end up when you're done talking. Do you have a call to some action you want people to take (such as donating money to your cause)? Do you want them to write to the school board to ask for healthier school lunches? What's your goal for this presentation? Do you want five new volunteers to sign up? What do you want to be ringing in your listeners' ears when you take your bow? Be as specific as you can. Write a powerful concluding sentence.

3. Now think about the points you need to make along the way to lead your audience members from your beginning to your ending. What information do they need to have in order to understand the whole story? What can you add to make it directly relevant to them? How can you make them feel what you want them to feel? Jot down some bullet points to help you remember your way so neither you, nor your listeners, get lost.

Believe it or not, you're done. You've written a speech! Now for the real work—practicing it!

HOW TO SAY IT

After you've figured out what you want to say, it's time to think about how you want to say it. Note that this doesn't matter very much if you don't have anything important to say. Focus on your message first! If you aren't clear and comfortable about your story, telling it will be more painful—for you and for the audience—than it needs to be. But once you have the content part nailed, you might be surprised how easily the delivery part comes together.

First, a bit about mechanics. It's okay to move while you're speaking—walking around the stage, using hand gestures, drinking water, and so on—but don't pace back and forth constantly like a caged tiger, bounce up and down or sway from side to side, twirl your hair, fidget with your pen, or do anything else that might become repetitious or distracting. Move your gaze around the audience while you speak, taking time to make eye contact with individuals as you go.

Use your voice—including both volume and pitch—wisely. Get louder for points that you want to emphasize. Don't let your sentences trail off at the ends and disappear. And the only sentences that should sound like questions—which rise in pitch at the end—are actual questions. Employ pauses when you want to stress a point or focus the audience's attention. Speak slowly, and clearly enunciate every sound.

Practice, practice, practice! Even the best speakers must practice, so don't think you're any different. Don't try to memorize the whole speech, though! Just give yourself some note cards with the major bullet points and key phrases you want to include, and then practice saying the words out loud. Thinking about what you want to say isn't enough, either. You have to actually say it—out loud—until it flows naturally. Practice out loud, with your note cards, all the way through, five times. Doing so will help you clarify and remember what you want to say, while still allowing you to be authentic and conversational during your delivery.

The TED conference videos are great examples of effective presentations. The organization does a good job helping the speakers prepare, and all of their presentations are available on the internet. Study some of their videos (ted.com/talks) to see what works well—and what doesn't—and then emulate the speakers who got it right while you're practicing your own speech.

Remember to breathe! Taking a deep breath not only calms you but also helps you slow down and gives your audience time to think. Your audience will not mind—if they even notice—that you paused to take a breath. And you'll be glad you did.

Tell yourself that you were invited because you have something to share. The people in your audience didn't come to watch you crash and burn, and they're not waiting to pounce on you if you fail. They are eager to hear what you have to say, and they want you to succeed. It's highly doubtful that you'll have an audience full of hecklers and bullies. Think of it as an audience of cheerleaders and friends instead.

Once again, smile! Not while you're giving grim statistics or spelling out the dire problem you're trying to solve, of course, but at least at the beginning and end of your speech. It will help put you—and the audience—at ease.

PRESENTATION SOFTWARE

In addition to your own speaking skills, many software programs or websites out there can help you create a slide deck to show to your audience while you're speaking. You could use Microsoft PowerPoint, Keynote, Google Drive, or Prezi.com, depending on what you are comfortable with and what you will have available when

you're preparing and delivering the speech. If you're thinking about using a slideshow at an event, talk to the organizers beforehand to make sure they will have everything you'll need, such as a projector and laptop setup, a screen, or maybe a whiteboard.

It's even more important, however, to first ask yourself if you should really use a slideshow at all. Remember that slides are visual aids, so only use them for things that are highly visual, and only if they will add value to your speech. If your slideshow might distract the audience from what you're saying, don't use it. Worrying about controlling your slideshow might prove to be a distraction for you, too, and make it harder for you to focus on giving your speech.

If you do use a slideshow, remember that you don't want your audience reading slides instead of listening to you, so don't fill your slides with too many words or make them too hard to read. Don't use slides as a crutch to help you remember your speech, because your delivery won't be as good as it could be. Most of all, don't think you can ever depend on your slideshow to help you give a great speech: things can and do go wrong, and the show must go on—with or without your slideshow.

It can be good to use slideshows, however, if you have photos or other images that will help illustrate the problem you are trying to solve, or your solution. Charts, graphs, or other visual representations can help make important data easier to understand and interpret. Make these slides as easy as possible to see and to read, even from the back of the room. Limit each slide to just one point, and get that point across in as few words as possible. Include your basic information—name, contact info, logo, and so on—as either the first or last slide, or both. Proofread your slides, and get someone else to proofread them as well, so you can be sure there are no mistakes. Finally, have a backup plan in case you can't use your slideshow for some reason.

NETWORKING

You'll likely have some time to mingle and network before or after you present. Those less formal interactions are great places to meet potential supporters. Remember that elevator pitch you wrote in chapter 5? This is the perfect time to use it! It's always a good idea to have an updated elevator pitch ready to go even when you're giving a different kind of presentation, since having your elevator pitch at the ready will make it easier for you to engage in conversations.

Chances are you're not alone in your passion or in the problem you're trying to solve, and networking and formal presentations are an aspect of marketing that can help you find others like yourself. Often, the most powerful and rewarding thing you can do is to connect with people who share similar ideas and enthusiasm, so don't be afraid to go out and find them and talk about all of the things you have in common. You never know . . . you might end up finding new volunteers, customers, donors, mentors, friends, and more.

And that is how change happens. One gesture. One person. One moment at a time.

Libba Bray, author, in her novel *The Sweet Far Thing*

| 14 |

Event Planning Boot Camp

Plans are worthless; but planning is everything.

Dwight D. Eisenhower, 34th president of the United States
of America, in a speech to the National Defense Executive
Reserve Conference on November 14, 1957

One of the most likely places you'll give a speech is at an event you and your team host yourselves. Putting on a concert, dinner, carnival, or other event is a great way to raise awareness of your venture and its cause. And even though hosting an event costs money, it has the potential to make even more money for your venture. Plus, planning an event can be a lot of fun!

Managing an event, however, also involves a great deal of time, organization, and risk. This chapter will help you decide if putting on an event is a good idea for your venture, and if so, show you how to do it.

In 2010, when she was just twelve years old, Adora Svitak was invited to speak at TED, a prestigious annual conference meant to share "ideas worth spreading." Adora's big idea was that thinking childishly—with bold ideas, wild creativity, and especially optimism—is a good thing, and that the world needs more of it, not less. She argued that everyone's big dreams deserve high expectations—children included—and that grownups should be willing to learn from children as well as teach them. Of course, right? Perhaps not surprisingly, though, she was the only young person there.

The experience had such an effect on Adora, however, that she decided to start her own offshoot conference to give other young people like herself a chance to share their own ideas worth spreading. That very same year, Adora and her friends hosted the first TEDxRedmond event, organized completely by kids for kids, in their hometown of Redmond, Washington.

The organizers, all under the age of sixteen, persuaded local company Microsoft to cosponsor the event and donate part of their corporate campus to serve as the venue. Generation YES also cosponsored the conference and provided youth volunteers and technical support for the lighting, sound, and video systems. In the end, eighteen young people from the around the country (including Jessica from chapter 5 in this book!) came to speak and perform. The crowd of over seven hundred attendees ranged in age from high schoolers down to seven-year-olds. All of the presentations were recorded and are still available on TEDxRedmond's website (tedxredmond.com). Talk about spreading ideas! Since then, the conference has grown every year and is now expecting more than a thousand attendees.

Adora admits that planning and organizing a large-scale event like this is extremely time-consuming and that it is sometimes difficult to handle having so many things on her plate. But the expectations of the audience members, plus the amount of work she and the committee have already put in, keep her going.

And the rewards have been worth all the hard work. In addition to learning to delegate tasks and trust others to see them through to completion, Adora's favorite aspect of the venture has been the camaraderie and bonding among the planning committee. "Members of my committee have been on my roof, known about crushes, played truth or dare together, and so much more," she says. "We may not all go to the same school, but by the end of the year our shared experiences have made us family." And, she's grateful to be a part of the larger community of ideas worth spreading, including the many presenters she's curated for TEDxRedmond as well as the other local organizations—like TEDxRainier and TEDxUofW—that have reached out to offer their support.

TEDxRedmond's annual event has shown thousands of young people that they can, in fact, start something that matters. How many of those young people—inspired by the TEDxRedmond speakers and the team itself—go forward now and touch the lives of others? It's impossible to say, of course, but it's clear that Adora's was an idea worth spreading.

TO EVENT, OR NOT TO EVENT?

Before you put in all the time and effort of planning an event, first make sure it's all going to be worth it. Take the following steps to help you explore whether hosting an event in the near future is a good idea for your venture.

1. Start by thinking about your goals for the event, and jot down your ideas in your journal. Is it to let people know about the problem and your solution? Is it to raise money? Is it to recruit volunteers? An event can accomplish all of

these things, of course, but knowing up front what the most important outcome is will help you make good decisions throughout the process.

2. Now consider the money it will take. How much can you afford to spend on this event? How will the event make money to support itself, and perhaps generate income as well? These questions will largely determine what kind of event you can even consider right now. A detailed budget of expenses and income will help keep you on track as you evaluate your options and bring one of them to life. Here's a sample event budget. Create your own now, filling it in with the amounts you think you'll spend and earn, and update it as you continue to plan and after the event has happened.

EVENT BUDGET

Income

DESCRIPTION	QTY	UNIT PRICE	ESTIMATE	ACTUAL
Ticket Sales	50	$100.00	$5,000.00	$4,500.00
Donations	10	$20.00	$200.00	$8,000.00
T-shirt sales	5	$15.00	$75.00	$225.00
Sponsorships	0	$50.00	$0.00	$100.00
Total Income			$5,275.00	$12,825.00

Expenses

DESCRIPTION	QTY	UNIT COST	BUDGET	ACTUAL
Food and Beverage				
Snacks	50	$6.00	$300.00	$300.00
Drinks	100	$2.50	$250.00	$300.00
Gratuity & Sales Tax (total 32%)			$176.00	$192.00
Total Food and Beverage			$726.00	$792.00

DESCRIPTION	QTY	UNIT COST	BUDGET	ACTUAL
Venue				
Facility Fee			$500.00	$500.00
Room Set & A/V Rentals			$150.00	$150.00
Total Venue			$650.00	$650.00
Entertainment				
Band		$500.00	$500.00	$500.00
Dance floor rental		$100.00	$100.00	$100.00
Total Entertainment			$600.00	$600.00
Registration				
Transaction Fees	50	$3.49	$174.50	$157.05
Credit Card Charges	50	$3.00	$150.00	$135.00
Total Registration			$324.50	$292.05
Event Support				
Programs and surveys	50	$2.50	$125.00	$125.00
Directional Signage	8	$2.50	$20.00	$12.50
Staging/Decorations			$80.00	$82.50
Name Tags	50	$0.50	$25.00	$22.50
Office Supplies (pens, tape, scissors, etc.)			$25.00	$10.00
Total Event Support			$275.00	$252.50
Volunteers				
Volunteer thank you gifts	25	$5.00	$125.00	$87.50
Total Volunters			$125.00	$87.50
Publicity				
Poster Printing	30	$2.00	$60.00	$67.50
Total Publicity			$60.00	$67.50
Miscellaneous				
T-shirts	25	$8.00	$200.00	$200.00
Parking fees				$15.00
Total Miscellaneous			$200.00	$215.00

DESCRIPTION	QTY	UNIT COST	BUDGET	ACTUAL
Total Expenses			$2,960.50	$2,956.55
Anticipated per person cost	50		$59.21	
Actual per person cost	45			$65.70

Profit or Loss

TOTAL PROFIT (INCOME MINUS ALL EXPENSES)		ESTIMATE	ACTUAL
		$2,314.50	$9,868.45

3. Then think about who will be on your event team. Do you have enough volunteers to coordinate the event planning? Can your team break into committees that will work well together on different aspects of the event? Does everyone involved have enough free time in their own schedules to devote to the planning effort? Do you have detail-orientated volunteers with the right kinds of skills to keep track of everything that goes into making an event happen? If you suspect the answer to any of these questions is no, this might not be the right time to organize an event.

If you're comfortable with your answers to all of the questions above about your goals, financials, and staff, then you're ready to dive into planning an event! Let's take a closer look at what goes into planning a successful event.

PLANNING

There are a few major task categories involved in event planning:

- Venue: Where will your event take place?

- Food and beverage: What will you serve your guests?

- Entertainment: What will guests do at your event?

- Publicity: How will people find out about your event?

- Volunteers: How will you get people to help before, during, and after the event? How will you manage them?

Let's talk more about each of these categories. Be sure to write in your venture journal about any ideas you have as you read through these guidelines. You might think of the perfect details, and you don't want to forget them!

VENUE

Deciding where to have your event depends on a few different factors. The first is how many people you expect will attend. This will affect what size facility you need as well as the features it must offer. If you're hosting a dance that you think will attract around fifty people, make sure your venue has a dance floor plus seating for that many people. If, like Adora, you're planning a conference for hundreds of attendees, you'll need a major conference center with lots of seating and some serious audio/visual equipment.

The date of your event will also affect your venue choice—and vice versa. For example, big hotels tend to book events a year or more in advance! Knowing the date, therefore, can help you eliminate some venues, as they may already be booked on the date of your event. And if you have some flexibility with dates, then determining the venue first may help you choose your date. When considering dates, research related school schedules and major events in your area to make sure there are no conflicts. Avoid holidays and other large community activities that may make it harder for people to attend your event.

The final factor to consider when choosing your venue is money. Nice hotels, for example, charge high fees for their meeting and banquet spaces. A church, school, or public hall, however, might give you a less fancy but significantly lower cost option. And if your event isn't going to be very large, consider asking someone if you can host it in his or her home or backyard.

FOOD AND BEVERAGE

Most events have food and beverages. Maybe you'll organize a neighborhood picnic and make it a potluck, where everyone brings a dish to share. Maybe you'll invite a food truck (or several) to park at your event and sell their wares to your guests. Or maybe you'll hire a caterer to prepare a full sit-down dinner, and you'll charge your attendees accordingly. For most events, food and beverage is a huge percentage of the overall expenses. Most venues that serve food won't let you bring your own, and they'll charge high prices for you to buy theirs. This can be used as a negotiation point, though. Committing to buy more food and beverages, for example, can help lower the cost of the venue. Just be sure you have all food and beverage costs documented in any contracts and accounted for in your budget.

ENTERTAINMENT

Most events have some kind of entertainment, something that makes people want to attend. It might be a featured speaker, music or a movie, or arts and crafts sales. You will probably have to pay something for this, although you may be able to get some things donated. Maybe you can find a photographer, for example, who will set up a photo booth in exchange for being able to hand out promotional materials. Or perhaps your cousin is in a band that hasn't yet performed in public and would like the opportunity to get on stage.

Whatever you decide, try to find opportunities to use the event to educate as well as entertain (and possibly fundraise). Most events mix these components in order to provide variety and hold people's interest. During breaks in the show, for example, people could give testimonials about the problem you're trying to solve or your venture's solution. You might also have a table with merchandise available for purchase. Maybe you can set up a silent auction that will run throughout the event. Whatever else you add, plan to include a short presentation about your venture, your mission, and your team. This will get people fired up about your venture—while they have a great time at your event.

PUBLICITY

If you want people to come to your event, you have to make sure they know about it. You'll need to spread the word far and wide, and invite about three times as many people as you hope to have attend. You can publicize an event using many of the methods discussed in chapters 11 and 12. It's best to use several so you get broader coverage. As part of the publicity, you may want to ask for RSVPs, collect registration information, or sell tickets. This will help you know how many people plan to attend and who they are, which can help you as you refine the details of your event. You might consider using a service like Eventbrite.com to facilitate the registration process.

VOLUNTEERS

Of course, you'll need your team to be fully engaged in event planning. You'll also most likely need additional volunteers, since planning and hosting an event takes so much time and effort. To begin with, designate someone from your team, most likely yourself, as the event coordinator. The event coordinator will have the big picture view of how the event is coming together and will oversee everything else.

Then, have someone on your team focus on recruiting volunteers. You'll need volunteers for setting up the event, keeping things running smoothly during the event, and cleaning up after the event. It can be useful to have your team and volunteers break up into committees, so a few people are in charge of each of the major task areas. Some key committees are ticket sales, publicity, entertainment, food and beverage, decorations, and fundraising activities.

When recruiting volunteers, keep in mind that people respond to incentives. "While I would like to claim that all of the volunteers I have procured are motivated by sheer altruism, that would be a lie," says Zach from Baking for Breast Cancer. "I have doled out the occasional gift card, not to mention [giving credit for] thousands of service hours (per my school's regulations, of course)." Giving volunteers a small token of appreciation, even if it's only public recognition, can go a long way toward establishing a solid volunteer base for future events, too.

Now that everyone has a committee, they know they each have a specific job to do and no one is stuck trying to do everything at once. Assigning these roles will go a long way toward ensuring a successful event.

CHECKLISTS

Build a checklist of tasks that need to be done and the dates they need to be done by, and keep close track of the timeline. This is one of the most helpful things you can do to guarantee your event's success. "Youth Ultimate Project's most successful fundraiser is our annual dinner and silent auction," says Chris. "Listing all of the action items for the event—from logistics to marketing—in a spreadsheet with a timeline helps us stay on task and productive." Below is a sample event planning checklist that you can adapt depending on your specific needs.

SAMPLE EVENT PLANNING CHECKLIST

DONE?	WHO?	WHEN?	CATEGORY?	DESCRIPTION
	Event Coordinator	ongoing	Event Planning	Oversee completion of task list assignments and update task list accordingly
	Team Leader	03/15/15	Event Planning	Reserve meeting room for first team event planning meeting and schedule meeting
	Team Leader, Event Coordinator	03/22/15	Event Planning	Determine agenda for team event planning meeting and send to team
	Team	03/25/15	Event Planning	Determine event date, format, and preliminary schedule
	Event Coordinator	03/26/15	Event Planning	Complete budget of planned income and expenses
	Team Leader	04/18/15	Venue	Reserve venue and sign contract
	Event Coordinator	04/19/15	Event Planning	Refine/update timeline and checklist
	Entertainment Coordinator	07/05/15	Entertainment	Start researching entertainment options and extending invitations
	Entertainment Coordinator	12/15/15	Entertainment	Reserve entertainment and sign contract
	Team Leader, Event Coordinator, Publicity Coordinator	12/15/15	Registration	Decide how people will register and reserve tickets
	Team Leader	12/15/15	Event Planning	Reserve meeting room for team event planning meeting and schedule meeting
	Team Leader, Event Coordinator	12/30/15	Planning	Determine agenda for team event planning meeting and send to team
	Publicity Coordinator	01/10/16	Registration	Test registration and ticket purchasing system
	Team	01/12/16	Event Planning	Make initial planning decisions and assign event tasks
	Publicity Coordinator	01/16/16	Publicity	Send event summary and information to webmaster for posting on website
	Publicity Coordinator	01/19/16	Registration	Send out email invitations and press releases
	Team Leader/Event Coordinator	02/01/16	Registration	Order any items that will be available for sale at the event
	Venue Coordinator	03/02/16	Venue	Determine table/seating requirements and work with venue on room layouts
	Food and Beverage Coordinator	03/02/16	Food and Beverage	Review menus for meals, snacks, and drinks
	Event Coordinator	03/07/16	Registration	Prepare post-event feedback survey questions for attendees and give to publicity coordinator

DONE?	WHO?	WHEN?	CATEGORY?	DESCRIPTION
	Entertainment Coordinator, Venue Coordinator	03/10/16	Registration	Send all A/V needs to venue staff and obtain cost estimates
	Publicity Coordinator	03/13/16	Publicity	Purchase event supplies such as name tags, banners, custom signs, etc.
	Publicity Coordinator	03/13/16	Publicity	Prepare all information to be printed for event attendees, including information about the venture and the event feedback survey, and give to designer
	Volunteer Coordinator	03/13/16	Volunteers	Write job descriptions for needed volunteer positions, including start and end times
	Volunteer Coordinator	03/14/16	Registration	Put out the call for additional volunteers
	Team Leader	03/24/16	Event Planning	Reserve meeting room for team event planning meeting and schedule meeting
	Food and Beverage Coordinator	03/28/16	Food and Beverage	Notify caterer of preliminary food and beverage orders
	Team Leader, Event Coordinator, Venue Coordinator	03/31/16	Venue	Carefully review and finalize the banquet event order (BEO), which is the venue's detailed plan for the entire event—including food and beverage, A/V needs, tables and chairs, etc.
	Venue Coordinator	04/03/16	Venue	Make list of all necessary signage and send to designer
	Team Leader, Event Coordinator	04/05/16	Event Planning	Determine agenda for team event planning meeting and send to team
	Publicity Coordinator	04/09/16	Publicity	Print final attendee materials
	Event Coordinator	04/11/16	Registration	Make name tags for attendees
	Team	04/12/16	Event Planning	Meet with team to go over event duties and finish any remaining tasks
	Team	04/18/16	Venue	Meet with venue staff for complete pre-event walk-through meeting
	Team	04/19/16	Event Planning	Have a fabulous event! Don't forget to collect feedback surveys when it's over.
	Event Coordinator	04/23/16	Event Planning	Write/deliver thank you notes to key vendors and contacts
	Event Coordinator	04/26/16	Registration	Share survey results with team and file for next time
	Team	04/27/16	Venue	Schedule, prepare for, and attend post-event meeting with venue staff

In My Experience

When I was coadvisor of my chapter of SCBWI, our most difficult task was organizing and hosting our annual conference. It was a two-day affair with over four hundred attendees, more than twenty speakers (most flown in from across the country), many different options, and special events. We hosted it at a hotel, provided food and beverages, charged different levels of fees, utilized over fifty volunteers, and had a full and complex schedule of entertainment, classes, and networking time.

What saved us were our checklists and spreadsheets. We had one master task list that we checked off as we completed items. We had many other spreadsheets for viewing our data and analyzing our needs. Perhaps even more important, we stored all of these documents on Google Drive, where our entire team could update them instantly from anywhere, so we'd always be on the same page. And we continued to reuse and improve these lists year after year, which saved us time and effort with every conference.

Over the course of the event, countless attendees thanked us for our hard work. People sent us emails for months afterward saying what a difference the conference had made to their careers and lives. Yes, putting on the conference was a gigantic undertaking that we worked on year-round. It was exhausting. But it was also thrilling, and more than anything, it was deeply rewarding. The more difficult the task, the better it makes you feel when you succeed.

HOW DID YOU DO?

Survey your attendees immediately after (or even during) the event to collect their feedback. Ask them how they felt about each of the major task categories (venue, food and beverage, entertainment, publicity, and volunteers), as well as what they thought about the event overall. You might want to look at the survey section in chapter 4 for a refresher on designing effective survey questions. Remember to keep most of the questions simple and easy to answer, but also leave some room for open-ended questions, such as "What did you like most about the event?" and "What do you think we could do better next time?" You could also include space for respondents to fill in their contact information and indicate whether or not they'd like to be added to your mailing lists.

Once you've collected the feedback from your attendees, schedule a team meeting to discuss how the event went. Share the results of the feedback survey, and discuss what went wrong during the planning and the event itself, as well as what went well. Take this opportunity to update the task checklist in case you missed anything before, so you'll have it ready for next time.

Speaking of next time, save all of your documents from the event. Not only will you want to have copies of the contracts in case you need to refer to them, but you'll also want contact information for everyone you worked with, and a record of which team members worked on which committees. You don't want to have to reinvent the wheel next time you organize an event, so make a folder and save everything from this one so you can find it easily.

IS IT REALLY WORTH IT?

After all that, you might be wondering if hosting an event is simply too much work to be worth the payoff. There's no doubt it's challenging, but as Adora advises other young changemakers, it's good to push yourself. "When you really go all out for something with no one telling you to . . ." she says, "it's the best feeling in the world."

Never doubt that a small group of thoughtful, committed individuals can change the world. Indeed, it is the only thing that ever has.

Often attributed to Margaret Mead, American cultural anthropologist

| 15 |

Covering Your Assets

Twenty years from now you will be more disappointed by the
things that you didn't do than by the ones you did do. So throw
off the bowlines. Sail away from the safe harbor. Catch the trade
winds in your sails. Explore. Dream. Discover.

Often attributed to Mark Twain,
nineteenth-century author

From the beginning, but especially as your venture grows and starts
doing more, you need to think seriously about protecting yourself:
personally, legally, and financially. Most of the advice in these areas
needs to be customized to your particular kind of venture, where
you're conducting your business, the groups you're working
with, and your own personal threshold for risk (as well
as that of your adult mentor and your parents!). Since I
couldn't possibly know or cover all the rules and guidelines specific to your situation in a book like this, we'll
first talk about risk management in general and then
some key topics for you to consider and investigate
on your own.

Profile
CHANGE THE WORLD
KIDS

The idea for Change the World Kids arose in 1998 after eight-year-old twins Phebe and Nika Meyers heard about a disaster abroad. Though devastated by their new understanding that lives can change in a heartbeat, Nika and Phebe realized that community members working together could help minimize the effects of tragic events. In response, they set up Change the World Kids, a network where kids in the Upper Valley area of Vermont could respond to calls for help from people in need.

Their first job was gardening and washing windows for an elderly couple incapacitated by illness. Since then, they've done all sorts of jobs like helping a family get back on its feet after a house fire and reconstructing a dam in a goose pond. One time a desperate woman called to say she'd had no heat for three days because her stack of firewood was frozen under the snow. Volunteers from Change the World Kids dug out the wood, delivered more, and stacked it in the woman's kitchen. But then they noticed that the woman had no bathroom, only one electrical outlet, plastic windows, and cracks in the walls where the cold outside air whistled through. So, over the course of a year and a half, they wired her house with electricity, put in a bathroom with a shower, replaced windows, sealed and insulated walls, and helped the woman get organized. "You've freed me to try and live a life here," the woman told them. "I feel like I got wings!" That kind of reaction makes Change the World Kids volunteers feel great.

Those volunteers have helped expand the Change the World Kids mission to include pursuing members' humanitarian and environmental interests both locally and abroad in areas including food justice, renewable energy, conservation, reforestation, disaster relief, youth empowerment, and more. "We saw opportunity everywhere," Nika and Phebe say.

And, since their efforts targeted the different interests of the group and gave everyone a chance to become a project spokesperson, volunteers saw opportunities as well. "Initially we reached out to our friends, who reached out to their friends," Phebe says. "The constant addition of new members brings new energy and enthusiasm to projects." She says that's a significant reason for the success of Change the World Kids. But they didn't stop there.

"I realized that if we became organized," Phebe says, "we would be more effective." So, Phebe and Nika got a lawyer and an accountant to donate their time helping with the process of incorporating Change the World Kids as an official 501(c)(3) nonprofit. The adult mentors also helped get Change the World Kids set up with a bank account and a budget. This gave the organization a strong foundation, and it received its 501(c)(3) classification in 2003.

Since then, Change the World Kids has hired an adult facilitator to work with project groups and committees and offer support as needed; raised more than $800,000; given more than ten thousand hours of service per year to local people in need; provided more than eleven thousand meals; distributed more than 160,000 trees; planted almost 9,000 trees; helped purchase seventy-three acres of land and protect more than three hundred acres of habitat in conservation agreements; and built a root cellar to provide a sustainable food storage solution for area food banks and a local school. It has been featured in local media, on the Voice of Leadership blog radio, in a PBS documentary, and in *People* magazine. It has grown to include additional chapters across the country. And Change the World Kids is still going strong.

RISK MANAGEMENT

Risk management is just what it sounds like—managing the risks involved with a given activity. You can't predict the future, of course, nor can you protect yourself from every possible threat out there. Yet you can take steps to prevent bad things from happening or prepare for them in a way that will keep you—and your venture—moving forward.

The key to successfully managing risks is balance. You don't want to ignore the risks completely, blindly hoping everything will work out for the best. That could have devastating consequences. But you also don't want to be so focused on things that might go wrong that you never get around to actually doing anything. It's easy to look at all the dangers and end up paralyzed. That's no good either.

The trick is to do things as you need them. Focus on the most likely and most catastrophic threats first, and then worry about the less likely and less dangerous threats later. Take some time to write in your venture journal to identify the most likely threats to your venture.

1. What activities will most people—you, your team members, volunteers, and people you're helping—be doing? Make a list with plenty of space between each activity.

2. Next to each activity, categorize it as physical, online, social, or other. For example, planting trees is clearly physical, and researching potential grant sources to be able to buy the trees to plant is an online activity.

3. Next, write what potentially bad scenarios could happen in each of those cases. In the example above, someone could hurt a hand or an ankle while planting a tree, or your venture's computer could get a virus while you're searching online.

4. Finally, write what simple preventative measures you could take. Maybe that includes showing people the correct way to hold the tree while planting it, so they are less likely to sprain a wrist.

By identifying potential risks in advance, you can be proactive about protecting yourself while still moving forward with your mission.

Now let's look at some categories of risk, including personal safety, laws, business registration, taxes, and insurance.

In My Experience

When my husband and I were looking for our first house, we had a definite maximum in mind for how much we were willing to spend. Still, the first three times our realtor took us out looking, he showed us houses that cost twice that amount! When we finally asked him what he was doing, he explained that he was trying to save us from ourselves. He was worried that we were looking at houses far below our income level and that we should maximize our possible real estate investment for the health of our long-term finances. He advised us to buy the most expensive house we could afford.

We explained that we wanted to be entrepreneurs, and that at some point in the future one of us would likely start a business while the other continued working and earned a steady income. We wanted to make sure we could keep making our mortgage payments on only one of our incomes, so we wouldn't put our financial stability at risk while we tried to start our own businesses. He said he'd never heard of such a thing but that it made sense, and he finally started showing us houses more in line with our desired price range.

Everyone has a different concept of risk and a different level of comfort with it. The realtor thought we were taking a risk by not putting our money into what he considered a stable long-term investment—a house. But we didn't want the risk of being saddled with an overly large monthly mortgage payment that would restrict our options down the road. To him, peace of mind was owning a great house. To us, peace of mind was money in the bank.

Fast-forward nearly twenty years later . . . both of us have our own businesses and are self-employed. We still live in a house smaller than what we could afford. But we both agree that having the safety net of a healthy savings account is better than having a bigger house—and it's a lot easier to keep clean.

PERSONAL SAFETY

Your first and foremost concern must be for your personal safety and that of your team. Always follow some basic common-sense rules:

1. Trust your gut. If something doesn't feel right, it probably isn't.

2. Use the buddy system so you always have backup in case things go wrong.

3. Make sure a responsible adult knows about your plans or goes with you to supervise.

Does this mean you shouldn't hand out hot meals to the homeless or travel to Africa to dig wells? No, of course not. Just check first with people who know the risks involved with those activities, or do other relevant research. Follow the advice you find, and take all recommended precautions.

LAWS

As I'm sure you already know, there are rules at many different levels to regulate all kinds of activities. Of course it's illegal to litter, but in some states, there are even laws about silly things like riding streetcars after eating garlic. Crazy! And when it comes to youth or business, you can be sure there are laws involved. Since you're dealing with both of those areas, be aware of the laws that apply specifically to you and your venture. Check with your school, city, county, state, and country to see what rules, ordinances, licenses, and laws might impact your activities. One place to start is to ask local businesses or established nonprofit organizations about their biggest legal issues. You can also search government websites or call government agencies if you have questions. And, of course, you can always consult an attorney.

Remember, rule-makers tend to be most concerned about the biggest issues. The smaller your venture is, the less likely it is to be breaking any rules (and the less likely anyone would notice if it accidentally did break a rule). But the bigger your venture grows and the more money it handles, the more likely you are to be affected by rules and regulations, and the more careful you will need to be to ensure you are doing everything right.

There's a lot to think about in this chapter. Keep in mind that you don't have to do everything mentioned here, and even professionals will have a hard time telling you what the perfectly correct answers are. Do the best you can, and know that most entrepreneurs out there are doing the exact same thing.

BECOMING OFFICIAL

You might have started your venture as a club, youth group, or association, and maybe that's just what you'll stay—which is fine. The bigger you grow, however, the more likely it is that you'll need to file official paperwork like registering for a business license, getting a tax ID number, or filing for a trademark. These things help establish your venture as a business, and the more you do to make your venture official, the more seriously people will take you. Remember, though, that not all of this official stuff needs to be done before you can start making a difference. If you're just getting started, just get started! Don't let the thought of all of these things on the future to-do list stop you from taking your first steps.

WHERE TO START

First, when do you need to register as an official business? There are a few key triggers that will make it necessary for you to register your venture. The specifics vary depending on where you live and what kind of activities your venture is engaged in, but some things to look at include how much money you're bringing in and if you're hiring any employees. If your venture operates in Seattle, Washington, for example, you must register with the state's Department of Revenue if you earn more than $12,000 per year, are required to collect sales tax or pay state taxes or fees, or are a buyer or processor of specialty wood products! You don't ever need to register with the county there, but you always need to register with the city.

Check the rules in your state, county, and city to make sure you understand what the particular thresholds are for you. Figure all this out well before you hit those limits, so you can register with the appropriate agencies and get all the licenses you need before it's too late. If you're in the United States, a great place to start is business.usa.gov/start-a-business. This simple online wizard will help you find the resources you need for your specific venture and location.

LEGAL STRUCTURE

Once you're ready to register your venture as a business, the next question is what business structure you want to adopt. Your venture can be a sole proprietorship, which means you're in charge—and completely responsible—for EVERYTHING, or it can be a partnership, meaning you share the responsibilities with one or more other people, which can get tricky. Those options are the simplest and easiest to set up, but neither offers you any personal protection from risks.

If you want to have more protection and be able to sell stock and have shareholders (which also means sharing ownership and control of your company), you'll want to register your business as a corporation. Also, if you want to be an official 501(c)(3) nonprofit (more on that in the next section), your business must be a corporation first. Corporations are the most expensive type of business structure to set up and require the most paperwork. If you want to go this route, you'll need to research the different kinds of corporations and look into the specific regulations for your location. I recommend seeking professional advice to make sure you get it right.

Luckily, there's another option called a limited liability company (LLC) that fits somewhere in between these two extremes. LLCs are legal entities that are separate from their owners, with their own money and responsibilities, so setting them up is more expensive and requires more paperwork than sole proprietorships or partnerships do. On the other hand, LLCs offer you some personal protection in case anything goes terribly wrong (such as your venture being sued) without requiring all the filings and other paperwork that a full corporation would. Because of that, the LLC is one of the most popular structures for small businesses.

PROFIT VS. NONPROFIT

The final step is deciding whether you're going to declare your venture as a for-profit or nonprofit business. For profit is just what it sounds like: your venture is intended to make money and can do whatever it wants with it, whether that means depositing it all in your personal bank account or donating it all to the homeless. This is the simplest kind of venture to start and to maintain, but your venture will have to pay taxes on all the money it brings in.

Nonprofit businesses, or charitable organizations, have more restrictions on how they can make money and how they can spend it, but they also have certain exemptions from paying taxes.

And one special kind of nonprofit corporation, a 501(c)(3), even allows donors to avoid paying taxes on the money they donate, provided the nonprofit keeps detailed records and files the right forms. If you're in the United States, websites like usa.gov/Business/Nonprofit.shtml and idealist.org/info/Nonprofits can help you decide whether you want your venture to be a nonprofit or a for-profit business. Note that becoming recognized as a 501(c)(3) corporation takes a great deal of time and effort.

If you're not ready to do everything necessary or simply can't wait to become a full 501(c)(3) yourself, you may want to look into getting a fiscal sponsor. These are nonprofit organizations that will help you collect and manage your donations, keep the necessary records, and file the required paperwork on your behalf. They typically keep a percentage of the funds raised in exchange for their services, but their help is often worth the cost, especially when you're just getting started. RandomKid has set up a 501(c)(3) umbrella (randomkid.org/content/66/501(c)(3)-umbrella.html) just for ventures like yours. You can also look at the directory of fiscal sponsors online at fiscalsponsordirectory.org/index.php or approach established nonprofits that work on causes related to your own to see if they'd be willing to sponsor you.

All of these are important decisions that will affect everything your venture does, so they deserve careful consideration. If you're in the United States, websites like business.usa.gov and LegalZoom.com can give you more information and help you assess the options for your specific case. You (and your parents) may also wish to ask an attorney or an accountant for advice. Just remember, it's allowed—and even quite common—to start out with one structure and then restructure later as your venture grows, when your needs change, or if you simply change your mind.

When you've decided on your structure and are ready to register your venture and apply for the necessary license(s), visit business.usa.gov (if you're in the United States) to help you find and file everything you need.

TAXES

If you're handling money—and you know you will be—you'll probably need to pay taxes, too, and you'll certainly need to file tax forms. There can be income taxes at the federal, state, county, and even city levels. There can also be sales taxes, use taxes, business taxes, and more. Once again, there are usually minimum incomes below which you don't have to worry, but they're different in every state and city, and you need to know what those minimums are and what to do when you cross them. Even if your venture is a nonprofit or you have a fiscal sponsor, you will still need to submit the required paperwork.

Paying income and sales taxes can add up to a significant amount of money for your venture, so it's worth considering taxes when you're deciding on your business structure, and you'll also need to include them in your budget. Once again, you (and your parents) may wish to consult a lawyer or an accountant for advice. And if you're in the United States, you can find all kinds of helpful information on the IRS webpage, irs.gov, and on your state's department of revenue site.

INSURANCE

Insurance is money that you pay regularly, when things are going well, to a company that will then cover your expenses if something bad happens. It might cost you a surprising amount, though! There are several different kinds of insurance, including:

- Liability insurance, which protects you financially if somebody gets hurt because of your venture's activities or if someone's property is damaged

- Homeowners' or renters' insurance, which will reimburse you if something happens to your property or your belongings inside your home or office, such as a theft or fire

- Auto insurance, which will reimburse you and possibly the other driver if your car is involved in an accident and can also pay the medical expenses of passengers, depending on your policy

Depending on where your venture operates and what kinds of activities you do, you may not need all of these. More important, you might already be covered under existing policies. For example, if you buy a new color printer for your venture and keep it at your house, it's probably covered under your parents' homeowners' or renters' insurance. If your venture is a school club and takes place on campus, its activities are probably covered under your school's liability insurance. Check with your parents and adult mentor to see what coverage you already have and what it makes sense to add in order to protect your resources.

OTHER FINANCIAL RISKS

Other kinds of things can go wrong, too. Your venture could end up losing money instead of making it. That's just one more reason to keep close track of your income and expenses, so you can minimize this risk. You don't want to go into debt or be careless with other people's money—or your own! Don't do things that you know aren't likely to succeed. Don't try to grow faster than your venture can support, either financially or in terms of your team's time or commitment. Think about the worst-case scenario, and make sure you can survive it. Yes, it takes money to make money, and some risk is unavoidable—you are changing the world, after all!—but always know what you're getting into and take calculated risks instead of major gambles.

Along with keeping an eye on your venture's financial records, you need to keep those records secure. Never give out passwords or PINs.

Limit the number of people who have access to your bank account and financial information, and store records and paperwork in a safe place. If you have a smartphone or computer, set a password lock on it so no one else can use it when you're not around. Protect your venture's identity like you would protect your own.

OTHER LEGAL ISSUES

You probably already have a name for your venture. The United States Patent and Trademark Office has information about how to trademark that name if you decide to do so. It costs money and takes time, so you might need to get some help with this step or wait until you're sure you need a trademark. It will take about three months for the government to approve your application, though, so don't wait too long. If you have a logo at this point, you can trademark the logo at the same time.

Another issue is copyright protection. If you're putting any original content—like writing, photos, drawings, or music—online or in printed materials, be sure to include a copyright statement. It can be as simple as "All content copyrighted by (your name or your venture's name)." Respect other people's copyrights, too. Just because words, pictures, movies, or songs are on the web doesn't mean you can use any of them for free. Check for Creative Commons licenses—a special designation that allows for some public sharing and use—or ask permission before using anything that isn't yours. If you don't have permission, it's stealing, plain and simple, and you could wind up in a heap of trouble even if you had good intentions.

WORKING WITH YOUNG PEOPLE

Finally, there are a few more issues you'll need to think about regarding working with young people. If you're hiring and paying people who are under eighteen, make sure you know the laws regarding child labor (in the United States, check youthrules.dol.gov).

If you're providing services to young people, make sure you obtain signed permission slips from their parents or guardians. Perform background checks on anyone who will be in direct contact with youth on behalf of your venture. You can run searches for criminal records on criminalsearches.com

Being aware of these issues will help protect you, your venture, and the young people you work with—whether team members or clients.

ASK FOR HELP WHEN YOU NEED IT

This kind of stuff can be tricky for any business owner, no matter how old or how experienced they are. Don't be afraid to look for assistance. "Ask for help, ask questions," Phebe and Nika recommend. "Put your heart into it and follow your dream while listening to the advice and support of those around you. Creating something knowing that others are behind you strengthens every part of your idea." And they add, "You can't do everything right away. It takes time to fully understand what an organization is capable of. Always be flexible, but stay true to yourself."

As their motto goes, "No one can do everything, but everyone can do something." Phebe says, "Even though I can't [completely] stop poverty, war, or rainforest destruction, I'm a changemaker."

The biggest risk is not taking any risk...In a world that's changing really quickly, the only strategy where you're guaranteed to fail is not taking any risk and not changing anything.

Mark Zuckerberg, founder and CEO of Facebook, in an interview with Jessica Livingston for Y Combinator's Startup School on October 29, 2011

| 16 |

Pairing Up for Perfect Partnerships

Everyone you will ever meet knows something you don't.

Bill Nye, the Science Guy, in a Reddit Ask Me Anything on July 27, 2012

Now that you're all official and have started on your way, you might be looking for ways to raise your venture's profile and increase its reach. One way to do that is to partner with another established organization. This is different from a legal partnership, which is a formal business structure where more than one person owns and operates the business. The partnerships we'll be discussing here are less formal ways for people and organizations to work together to achieve their separate but related goals.

There are probably other organizations with goals similar to your venture's goals or that you and your team would like to support or be supported by. Partnering with one or more of those organizations can help everyone involved by enhancing credibility, sharing promotional efforts and audiences, and distributing costs more efficiently.

Profile
NEVERSECONDS

Martha Payne from Argyll, Scotland, never set out to be a changemaker. She simply wanted to be a journalist, reporting on the way things were.

After a school assignment in which she wrote a pretend newspaper article about the sinking of the *Titanic*, nine-year-old Martha told her father she wanted to write like that every day. They talked about what she could write about, and he helped her set up a blog.

One thing Martha knew she could write about was her school lunches. She had them practically every day, after all. She called her blog NeverSeconds—not because she never wanted seconds, but because she wasn't allowed to have any, even if she was still hungry. Her blog wasn't intended to be an exposé, and Martha wasn't complaining or advocating for any specific changes. She was just reporting: taking a photo of her meal and rating it on taste, portion size, nutrition, and—ew!—the occasional strand of hair. She even got the school's permission. Her first post went up on April 30, 2012.

After Martha's first few posts, her dad posted a link on his Twitter account. Less than four hours later, the blog had been visited more than ten thousand times. Readers assumed it was a campaign to improve school lunches and jumped on board. Newspapers and television stations called. Then professional chef Jamie Oliver sent Martha a tweet of support. NeverSeconds went viral.

The school council grew defensive at what they perceived as an attack. They retaliated, forbidding Martha from taking any more photos. Martha was confused and disappointed: she liked blogging, but she didn't want to get in trouble or hurt anyone's feelings. Her supporters were outraged: they fanned the publicity flames even higher. Eventually, under much scrutiny and pressure from the public, the council relented and Martha started blogging again.

When NeverSeconds had more than fifty thousand readers per day after just a few months, Martha decided to put it to work doing good. In previous years, she and her brother had helped her grandparents stuff backpacks with donated school supplies for an organization called Mary's Meals. The previous year, Martha had started a club called Charity Children, which held a craft sale at her school and raised enough money for Mary's Meals to feed seven children school lunches for a whole year. And in the impoverished African countries where Mary's Meals worked, that was often the deciding factor in whether or not a child went to school at all. Since her blog was a huge hit, Martha and her dad made a page on JustGiving.com where Martha's blog readers could donate to Mary's Meals directly. Then she included information about Mary's Meals in one of her posts and added the link to NeverSeconds.

So far, Martha's JustGiving page has received more than 7,500 donations, raised more than $200,000, and built an entire kitchen in Lirangwe, Malawi. Martha says, "NeverSeconds started about my school dinners, but now it is about every child's school dinners" (that's what they call lunch in Scotland). "Around the world, children are helping those with less, and we couldn't do that without Mary's Meals."

WHY PARTNER?

The key to finding a good partner is understanding that the relationship must go both ways. You have to be willing to give something to your partner in order to get something in return. It won't necessarily be an even exchange, but both sides must feel like they are gaining something. For this reason, it's best not to look for a partner until you've been operating for a while and have something of value to offer.

That doesn't mean it will be difficult for you or will require much sacrifice on your part. By partnering with your venture, organizations can enhance their credibility with young people, improve their outreach to youth, demonstrate commitment to their community, and earn public goodwill. They may also benefit from your unique knowledge, skills, and experiences. Don't underestimate your venture's value.

Know what you're looking for in a partner, too. As you evaluate potential partners, consider how well they might be able to meet your needs as well as how you can help them. Martha's blog raises money for Mary's Meals, but she gets something in return. First, she gets to ask them for advice on how to do things. Second, they understand that she doesn't want to be famous and they don't pressure her to do anything she isn't comfortable with. Perhaps most important, though, is the personal reward Martha gets from the partnership. "Our Mary's Meals kitchen is called the Friends of NeverSeconds Kitchen, and every day it feeds two thousand children. That puts a huge smile on my face," Martha says.

In My Experience

One of my other books is about a man from Ghana. He was born disabled, and at the time, people with disabilities in Ghana were treated poorly. As a young man, he got himself a bicycle and rode it—using only one leg—almost four hundred miles all around his country to show everyone there that disabled people can do great things. Later, he founded a school where disabled children could learn for free. I was inspired by his actions, and I wanted to tell his story.

This is a great case for a partnership, don't you think? The more books about him that I sell, the more people will know about him and his cause. The more people who hear him speak about his accomplishments, the more people will be interested in buying my book. When I am out promoting my books, I am also promoting his cause. When he is out speaking about his cause, he is also speaking about my book. Hopefully, we'll even find opportunities to speak together at the same events!

I'm not sure yet how much we'll be able to do with this partnership, but I'm looking forward to seeing how we can work together to help both of us accomplish our goals.

WHERE TO FIND A PARTNER

Now it's time to choose a potential partner. Start by thinking about organizations that address a problem similar to what your venture does. If your venture is tackling an environmental issue, for example, you may want to partner with a larger, more established environmental organization.

Also consider organizations that are reaching out to the same audience—either the audience you're helping or the audience you're asking for support. If your venture is addressing the problem of homelessness, partnering with an organization addressing hunger might benefit you both. Or, if your venture helps senior citizens care for their pets, you might want to partner with an organization that helps senior citizens file their taxes, or one that helps people with AIDS care for their pets, or both!

Sometimes, the best partnerships don't seem related at all. Say your venture teaches children how to knit. You can raise money to keep your venture profitable by selling the knitted items, but you can also donate some of the proceeds (whether in the form of cash or knitted items like baby blankets) to a local hospital. Teaching kids how to knit has nothing to do with hospitals, but giving back to the community in this way raises awareness of your venture, encourages people to buy your items, and gives the kids a powerful incentive to keep knitting.

Making a mind map of your issue, the people involved with it, and the organizations surrounding it might help you brainstorm ideas for whom to approach about partnering. A mind map is a way to organize your brainstorming and associate related ideas together.

1. Start by writing your main issue in the middle of a blank page in your journal and circling it.

2. Now think about a person, group, or organization related to your issue. Write it down near your main issue and circle it. Connect the two with a line.

3. Continue thinking about people, groups, or organizations related to your issue and making branches to connect them to your main issue.

4. Now, go back and make subbranches out from those nodes, thinking of people, groups, or organizations related to those first groups that you thought of.

5. From your subtopics, branch out even farther, if you can, by adding supporting details as you think of them.

Here's what an example of what a mind map might look like. ⟶

HOW TO GO ABOUT IT

Once you've identified some potential partners, it's time to do more research. Find out everything you can about them by looking at their websites, chatting with people who might be involved with them, and searching for press releases or other news reports about them. Pay special attention to whether or not they already have partnerships with other organizations and how you might complement their programs.

If you have an organization on your list that still looks like a good match, look for someone in the organization whose title indicates she is in charge of partnerships. Call or email her. If you can't find someone specifically in charge of partnerships, look for job titles dealing with development, strategy, outreach, or public relations. Of course, you can always try someone higher up like a director or CEO, but depending on the size of the organization, those people may be too busy to reply. If you can't find a specific contact that seems to make sense, just use the organization's general contact information. Briefly introduce yourself, your venture (there's your elevator pitch again!), and why you think the organization might want to partner with you. Invite the person to talk about it further with you, and propose some times when you'd be available.

MIND MAP

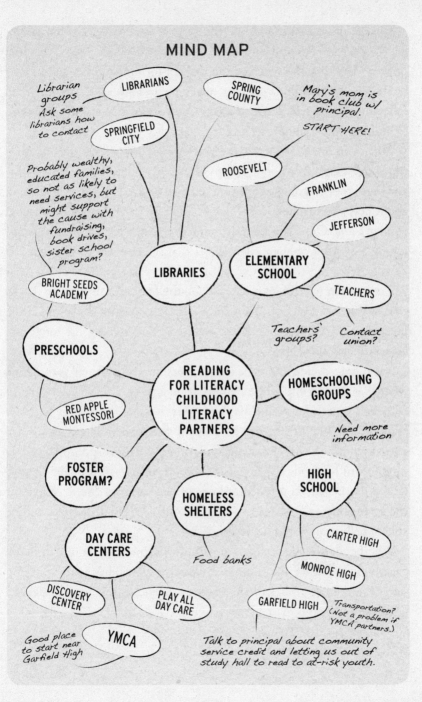

Librarian groups
Ask some librarians how to contact

LIBRARIANS

SPRING COUNTY

Mary's mom is in book club w/ principal.

START HERE!

SPRINGFIELD CITY

ROOSEVELT

FRANKLIN

JEFFERSON

Probably wealthy, educated families, so not as likely to need services, but might support the cause with fundraising, book drives, sister school program?

LIBRARIES

ELEMENTARY SCHOOL

TEACHERS

BRIGHT SEEDS ACADEMY

Teachers' groups?

Contact union?

PRESCHOOLS

READING FOR LITERACY CHILDHOOD LITERACY PARTNERS

HOMESCHOOLING GROUPS

RED APPLE MONTESSORI

Need more information

FOSTER PROGRAM?

HIGH SCHOOL

HOMELESS SHELTERS

CARTER HIGH

DAY CARE CENTERS

MONROE HIGH

Food banks

DISCOVERY CENTER

PLAY ALL DAY CARE

GARFIELD HIGH

Transportation? (Not a problem if YMCA partners.)

Good place to start near Garfield High

YMCA

Talk to principal about community service credit and letting us out of study hall to read to at-risk youth.

Keep in mind that the people you contact are likely very busy, might be volunteers, and probably don't know much about you. Their first priority should be their own missions—not forming partnerships. Don't be surprised if they don't get back to you. Give it a week or two and then follow up. If you still don't get a reply, don't take it personally. Move on to another potential partner and try again.

When you finally do land a meeting, ask questions. Ask the organization's representatives about the problem they're trying to solve, why, and how they're going about it. Find out what they need, and think about how you can help. Don't be afraid to give suggestions or advice if you have any. Or, if you have the same problems they do, suggest working together to solve them. Remember that the best way to get what you need is to ask for it. Be honest with potential partners, both about what you're looking for in a partner and about what you can provide. Make sure to leave your business card and press kit with them at the end of the meeting, and ask if you can add them to your mailing list for future communications.

If you both decide to pursue the partnership, the next step is to decide what that partnership will look like. It may be as simple as agreeing to add each other's logos and links to your websites, or it may be more complicated, like organizing an event together. It might even involve a legally binding contract about something like fiscal sponsorship. You might want to decide the time period in advance, or you might want to let the partnership continue until one of you wants to end it. Whatever the arrangements, make sure they suit your needs and that you will be able to deliver on your responsibilities.

Whether or not you go forward with the partnership, be sure to thank everyone for taking the time to discuss the possibility with you. You never know when things might change or come back around, so leave a good impression no matter what happens.

FINAL THOUGHTS

When they work out, partnerships are win-win propositions, and having a solid one—or several—can help your venture achieve its goals by spreading out your support system. In her book, *NeverSeconds*, which she cowrote with her dad, Martha said, "It's been awesome. I never knew I could write so much or help so many kids until I tried."

Strong partnerships are one important factor in the stability of your venture as it grows and changes. Martha isn't actively blogging anymore, for example, but donations to Mary's Meals are still coming in through her JustGiving page. In the next chapter, we'll talk about sustainability and other ways your venture can succeed long-term.

If you can dream it, you can do it.

Tom Fitzgerald, Walt Disney Imagineer, written for the
Horizons attraction at Walt Disney World's Epcot Center

Making It Last

Be of good cheer. Do not think of today's failures, but of the success that may come tomorrow. You have set yourself a difficult task, but you will succeed if you persevere; and you will find a joy in overcoming obstacles.

Helen Keller, deaf and blind author, political activist, and lecturer, in an address to the American Association to Promote the Teaching of Speech to the Deaf on July 8, 1896

Just like NeverSeconds, many of the other ventures profiled so far are still operating even though their founders have gone on to do other things. Others are planning for or are already in the process of a leadership change. Adora (chapter 14), for example, told me that her next challenge with TEDxRedmond was to transition the event to new leadership. "It's a strange thing to say that your goal is to make yourself replaceable," she says, "but that's really going to be my way of measuring if I've been successful. If TEDxRedmond can sustain itself as a great, authentically youth-run event for many years to come without me there, I'll know I've done a good job."

One of the things that differentiates an entrepreneur from an ordinary businessperson is the ability to create something that will last long after his or her involvement with it ends. Building that kind of sustainability can also be one of the trickiest things to do. Founders bring so much energy and passion to an organization that it can be hard for anyone involved to imagine a future without the founder present. Change happens, though, especially when young people are involved! Who knows what your life will bring down the road? This chapter will show you some ways to help make leadership transitions smoother and easier for you, for your team, and for your venture.

Profile

EVERYBODY DANCE NOW!

When Jackie Rotman was twelve years old, she performed a hip-hop routine for teenagers with disabilities . . . until the music suddenly stopped. Not knowing what else to do, she and her fellow performer invited the audience onstage to show off some of their moves. "All of these kids looked so confident and happy," Jackie told *Glamour* magazine. "That's when I realized that I could use dance to empower people."

When she also realized that gang violence, obesity, and low self-esteem threatened her Santa Barbara, California, neighborhood, Jackie felt compelled to take action. Jackie opened a bank account, got liability insurance, applied for grants, and raised money with the help of her mentor, Julie McLeod of the Santa Barbara Dance Alliance. "She played an especially instrumental role in helping me set up Everybody Dance Now! in its early stages," Jackie says.

By the time she was fourteen, Jackie and three other young dancers from her studio were providing free weekly hip-hop dance classes. Lower-income children learned how to dance at local youth centers, after-school programs, and homeless shelters, and then they performed for people at senior centers and community events. "Once we began, opportunities and ideas continued to present themselves," Jackie says.

"Don't hesitate because you feel like you have to have the whole model or long-term vision figured out and on a massive scale. You can start small. Just start!" She adds that after almost eight years of steady work, Everybody Dance Now! has achieved things she never even envisioned when she began the project.

One of the biggest challenges Jackie faced with Everybody Dance Now! came long after the venture was up and running, even though she'd planned for it. Sustainability—from a leadership standpoint—was an issue Jackie thought about right from the beginning. "I wanted Everybody Dance Now! to be something that continued on after I went to college," Jackie says. Since Jackie graduated from high school, Everybody Dance Now! has gone through several leadership transitions at its original Santa Barbara chapter. "While I was in high school," Jackie explains, "I trained a younger high school student to codirect the chapter with me when I went away to college. Then, when she was getting ready to go to college, I recruited six young leaders who could take the chapter on as a team." Everybody Dance Now! has since transitioned through three different Santa Barbara directors and maintains a team of six to ten young people, who carry out various responsibilities and gain skills and confidence along the way.

Everybody Dance Now! has also grown to include eight chapters in different cities across the nation. "We try to educate our chapter leaders about succession planning and ways of preparing for leadership transitions of their chapter," Jackie says. "They've got to continually be identifying and cultivating talented people who can be future leaders for the chapter, providing proper training and support for these emerging leaders, and ensuring the chapter has sufficient resources, advisors, and foundations to be sustainable throughout leadership changes. Because most of our chapters are youth led, leadership transition and turnover presents a challenge for most chapters every one to four years."

Then, there's the overall leadership at the national level. "We're now working to put in place more structures so Everybody Dance Now! can be sustainable," Jackie says. "We need to build a strong and engaged board of directors, get Everybody Dance Now! to a sufficient budget size so that we can afford a full-time national executive director and future staff who support our chapters, plus put in place the proper training and programmatic structures to be effective." Now that Jackie has graduated from college, she's gone back to Everybody Dance Now! and is devoting herself fully to completing that effort.

SUSTAINABILITY

When most people today hear the word *sustainability*, they think it refers to our impact on the environment. That's not the kind of sustainability I'm talking about. I'm talking about setting up your venture so it can sustain itself far into the future—with or without you. Sustainability comes into play as an organization grows and becomes too much for one person to handle, requiring the leader to take a less direct role and delegate more tasks to more people. Sustainability is also important when you want to move on to something new or you have a life change—such as going off to college or getting a full-time job—that prevents you from managing the day-to-day activities of your venture.

These things will most likely occur after your venture has been running for a long time, but there are many good reasons to think about sustainability early on. Sharing the leadership load from the beginning will allow you to manage your own time better throughout the life of the venture and will give more people a chance to become personally invested in its success. Your venture will be more likely to win grants and receive donations if it's a long-term project instead of a one-time activity. The more active volunteers you have and the more people who are interested in your venture, the more you'll be able to get done.

In these ways, making your venture sustainable from the beginning allows you to increase your impact and helps ensure that your efforts will not be in vain.

AVOIDING BURNOUT

Even if you don't pass the torch with your venture, you need to be able to maintain your passion for and dedication to your cause. Make sure you can balance your other commitments without wearing yourself out. The same goes for your team members and volunteers. Burnout—exhaustion to the point of disinterest—is bad for you physically and mentally, and it's bad for your venture. Burnout can affect anyone, and it's nothing to be ashamed of, but you can take steps to prevent it.

One of the best ways to prevent burnout is to take time to rest. If you've just hosted a major event, for example, don't jump right into a media campaign. Give yourself—and your team members and volunteers— some time to relax for a while. Step away from your venture and focus on other activities that you enjoy. Zach, from Baking for Breast Cancer (chapter 11), was active in athletics, choir and drama, and Model United Nations while running his venture. He was also involved in the student advisory board and served as a peer tutor at his school. He took AP classes and earned a top score on his SAT. He even taught classes at his temple. How did he do it all? "Having such diverse activities helps me stay on track," he says. "When I'm tired of schoolwork, switching to Baking for Breast Cancer work is a welcome change. Likewise, athletics are very time consuming but more physically demanding, whereas Baking for Breast Cancer is more psychologically taxing." Although he was very busy, having a balance of difference kinds of activities kept Zach going.

Another way to prevent burnout is to spend time hanging out with your team just for fun, with no other venture-related agenda. Celebrate all you've accomplished together. You've earned it! That togetherness and bonding is key to keeping your team members—and yourself— engaged and enthusiastic about your venture now and in the future.

HAND-OFF

Whether you burn out or not, you're probably going to want to move on to something else eventually. So, what can you do from the beginning that will make the leadership transition easier when the time comes? First, even though it may be your idea and your passion that gave birth to the venture, try to put your ego aside and involve your team members as much as possible. Seek their input, involve them in brainstorming, and discuss ideas together. Form committees or task forces, and give each group leader ownership of her piece of the puzzle. Give everyone positive feedback on the things that go well so they'll be more likely to repeat them. And on the flip side, always own up to your weaknesses and mistakes.

Second, save everything. Keep detailed, organized records of all of your plans as well as what actually resulted from them. Stop to evaluate your actions as a team as you go along, and store those evaluations, too. This will create a kind of living history of your venture, so new people coming in will have something to look at and build from. They can learn from your experience even if you can't remember, don't have time to talk about it, or have long since moved on.

Third, allow team members to try on different roles, including yours. Encourage shadowing, letting one team member observe another team member (or you) to learn the ropes of what that job entails. The more people can move around, the more coverage you'll have, and the venture won't be devastated if someone leaves unexpectedly.

Fourth, look outside your organization for assistance when you need it. Similar to having people inside your team familiar with different roles, having the right professionals and partnerships in place will facilitate periods of change. An accountant who is familiar with your venture's transactions can help a new leader get up to speed quickly on the financial side of things. A partner who has helped you plan events in the past can get a new team up and running quickly for the next event. Having people in the know who are still involved with your venture—both internally and externally—will help ensure smooth leadership transitions.

Finally, take promotion seriously. The more you get the word out about your venture, the more people will want to be involved with it. And the bigger pool of volunteers you have to draw from, the better you'll be set up for long-term success.

In My Experience

When I became involved with SCBWI Western Washington, there were three competent leaders at the helm (two advisors and one assistant advisor) plus a team of key volunteers. The idea was that only one of the three leaders would step down at a time so there'd always be continuity. In addition, the assistant advisor was essentially training to become an advisor, so there was always someone coming up through the ranks. It was a fine sustainability plan . . . or so we all thought.

Due to life events (and perhaps a little bit of burnout), all three of those leaders quit at the same time, throwing the thriving organization I loved and valued so much into a potentially fatal situation. Three of us who'd been key volunteers timidly stepped forward and assumed the leadership roles. We hadn't really worked together before, as we were on separate projects, and we had no idea what we were getting ourselves into, but we were not willing to let our regional SCBWI chapter die. Our main goal was simply to not screw things up.

Fortunately, the previous leadership team left us everything we needed to succeed. Even though they weren't leading anything anymore, all three of them transitioned into key volunteer roles so they were still involved when we needed them. They were available for meetings and phone calls to give us advice on important decisions. Everything they'd ever done was well documented and explained, including templates, checklists, and instructions. And all of the outside organizations we'd been working with for things like banking, events, and membership databases remained the same, so we didn't have to re-create anything from scratch.

We spent the first year mostly just getting up to speed on everything, but pretty soon we were changing things up and putting our own mark on the programming. As we got more comfortable, we added new events and offerings. SCBWI Western Washington grew and prospered, and we received good feedback on our work.

Still, we failed in one important way . . . we didn't adequately address how the chapter was going to sustain itself in the future. We'd stepped into demanding roles and pushed them even further. We let our commitments grow faster than we, or the team, could handle. We burned out, and so did the leaders who came after us who tried to shoulder the same burden. Recruiting new leaders became impossible, so the entire organization was forced to stop and re-evaluate what it was doing, what was most important, and how it was going to get it done with the volunteers available. It was a painful realization and a time-consuming process, and the results probably disappointed and confused many of our members.

Still, SCBWI Western Washington's members are grateful for the services the organization does provide, and the volunteers are committed to keeping the organization going in a more sustainable form. With all that going for it, I'm confident the chapter will continue to deliver on its mission for years to come.

FRESH MEAT

Recruiting new volunteers is similar to building your original team. You might want to look over chapters 5 and 6 again to help you remember how to bring new people into the fold. Here's a short summary:

- Ask! Get the word out about your venture. Display volunteer sign-up sheets. Make it clear what kind of help you need.

- Be organized and don't waste people's time, but have fun and reward them for showing up.

- Make sure new people feel welcomed, included, and appreciated.

- Teach new volunteers what you've already learned by sharing your history and records as appropriate.

Keep in mind that there are both benefits and challenges to working with teen volunteers. As you well know, young people have many interests and commitments competing for their time. Their lives are in a constant state of change, so they transition through different roles frequently and need to build new relationships constantly. Plus, like you, most of your volunteers will be learning and applying new skills as they go.

Jackie knows about these problems firsthand, as she's seen them all with Everybody Dance Now! Still, she says the good outweighs the bad. She points out that youth volunteers make an organization easily scalable. "We don't have to raise hundreds of thousands of dollars every time we want to open a new chapter—instead, we mobilize several incredibly motivated young people and their advisors to build their chapters and recruit other people." Being youth led can also become an explicit part of your venture's mission. As Jackie puts it, "We're dedicated not just to helping the students in our program, but also to positively transforming the lives of the young people who lead our programs and learn a great deal from it—and hopefully become impassioned about public service—in the process."

Having young leaders also distinguishes your organization, she says. "It helps us connect with our students, who are close in age to our organization, and it makes us different. We're able to utilize this with various funders and supporters to our advantage." Finally, recruiting young volunteers means team members are doing what they do because they love it. Otherwise, they would leave. "This leads to an incredibly passionate, caring, and motivating group of people on the team," Jackie says. And that's what you need more than anything else.

THE MULTITUDES

As you promote your venture for fundraising as well as for other purposes, you'll constantly add new people to your mailing lists. Keep in touch with all of those subscribers by periodically sending out relevant information, and you'll have a steady stream of new volunteers to keep things running. If you have a specific job that you need a volunteer for, include a call for help in your regular member communications. You never know when someone mildly interested in your venture might be ready to get more involved. Review chapters 11, 12, and 13 if you think you need to be more active with your promotion.

IN IT FOR THE LONG HAUL

Changemakers and social entrepreneurs build something that lasts. They aren't your typical one-time-only do-gooders, and you're not either. You can stay at the helm and be effective for as long as you wish, as long as you take good care of yourself and your team. And, when you're ready to pass the torch, you know how to make it a successful transition.

Still, no matter how much you plan, surprises are bound to come up. "I think being an entrepreneur is one of the most creative pursuits you can have," Jackie says. "The minute you accomplish one goal you've been working toward, you're already on to the next thing—growing and evolving the vision into truly beautiful interactions, outcomes, and processes that can continue to make a valuable difference in people's lives." She says her life changed when she started Everybody Dance Now! It gave her something to focus on—a clear goal and vision to further develop.

She gained a sense of purpose, direction, and excitement that allows her to channel her energy into an area she's passionate about.

And you probably have, too!

There is no need for temples; no need for complicated philosophy. Our own brain, our own heart is our temple; the philosophy is kindness.

His Holiness Tenzin Gyatso, the 14th Dalai Lama,
in *Dalai Lama: A Policy of Kindness*

| 18 |
Now What?

A new type of thinking is essential if mankind is to survive and move toward higher levels.

Albert Einstein, physicist and winner of the 1921 Nobel Prize in Physics, in the *New York Times* on May 25, 1946

Where you go from here is up to you. You've acquired new skills, racked up useful experiences, made connections, and learned a bit more about who you are and what's important to you. You're a change-maker, and you're on your way.

Profile

PROJECT BELIEVE IN ME

In 2011, Alex Horsey noticed there were many news stories about bullying, especially bully-related suicide. He worried that young people were only hearing the unhappy endings. While he knew it was important to respect those who felt there was no other way out, he also wanted young people to know they weren't alone in their struggles. He'd been bullied since elementary school, and he knew things could get better. Alex, then a junior in high school, founded Project Believe in Me to counterbalance the media's portrayal of the bullying problem.

Based in Portland, Oregon, Project Believe in Me allows people from anywhere in the world to submit a letter about their own experiences with bullying to the organization's website (projectbelieveinme.org). The posts can be anonymous, or not—it's up to the letter writer—but either way, the project gives the victims of bullying a chance to speak out and be heard.

Once approved by Project Believe in Me staff, the letters are categorized by topic to help readers find letters most applicable to their situations. The letters are then posted online for all to see. Looking through these letters about others' experiences offers readers from around the world hope that they can make it through whatever bullying situations they find themselves in.

Alex says several things helped him launch the project. First, he turned to DoSomething.org, which helps connect and support teens interested in social change. The online resources there helped kick-start his journey. Then, once he started getting out and promoting the project, he met Oriana Quackenbush, who sits on the board of the Oregon Safe Schools and Communities Coalition, which lobbies for statewide anti-bullying policies and reports on school district compliance. She became the adult mentor for Project Believe in Me and helped the youth-led organization grow and evolve. Portland itself has been supportive of the project, too. Project Believe in Me received two grants from the City of Portland's Youth Action Grant program, which puts funds in the hands of young people to empower them to create change around issues that are important to them.

Alex says the most challenging aspect of launching Project Believe in Me was dealing with some of the attitudes he faced. "There's something about a sixteen-year-old introducing [himself] as an executive director that some find to be more funny than serious," he says. To get through difficult times, he focuses on the people he's trying to help. "In the world of statistics, grant applications, and such, the value of reaching one person gets pushed aside," he says. But then he'll read a letter someone wrote and know that reaching that person made a difference. "That's what keeps me going," he says.

In the future, Alex hopes Project Believe in Me will continue to grow and expand its reach, and he also wants to help other young people find the resources and encouragement they need to start their own ventures. Alex is trying to implement his own grant program via Project Believe in Me, and he hopes to one day become an adult mentor to provide other young people with the same kind of guidance and support that he received.

And he's well on his way. In addition to studying Community Development in college, Alex was a member of the DoSomething National Youth Advisory Council for two and a half years. "Being exposed to such a tightly bonded group of young people with the same change-making mind-set was one of the most impactful experiences I've had in my life," he says. "I've always believed that young people could create change, but this was the first time I had seen action of that caliber firsthand."

Alex advises against trying to hide your youth. "Be proud of it!" he says. "Say, 'Hey, I'm sixteen, and I'm starting this because it's important. Here's how you can help.'" He says it's important to remember that you are not alone as a young changemaker. "Don't let anyone tell you that we're the 'leaders of tomorrow,'" he says. "You're a leader and the changemaker of *today*."

BUT, WHAT ABOUT . . . ?

There are, of course, many other issues you care about besides your venture's main focus. You might feel bad for choosing one problem over all the others out there or wish there was more you could do. Fortunately, you can still have an indirect impact on other issues in the way you manage your venture. Through the decisions you and your team make every day, your venture can advocate for many different issues and groups besides just the ones you've chosen to focus on. If your venture's core mission is protecting baby seals on the beaches, for example, then you will probably avoid littering the beach while you stand guard. If your main goal is educating young children whose parents can't afford preschool, you might end up becoming involved in literacy programs for adults.

More and more companies today realize that doing good is good business and are subscribing to a three-pronged approach that balances profit with people and the planet, and so can your venture. Doing the right thing helps you earn respect and goodwill. If you show that you act ethically and responsibly, people will trust you and your venture. In addition, the decisions your venture makes allow it to set a good example for other companies, organizations, governments, and individuals and show them that they can choose to do good, too.

So, when you're making your normal day-to-day decisions, think about things like fair trade, living wages, and workers' rights. You may want to buy local and support independent businesses and artisans whenever you can, or consider how your choices affect the environment and try to minimize your carbon footprint at your next event. Made with care, each seemingly small decision can have a considerable impact in your community and throughout the world.

Be conscientious whenever possible, but don't become bogged down or overwhelmed, either. It's easy to get paralyzed when you have too many things to worry about, so be sure all of your efforts are squarely focused on and support your goal. Don't ever sacrifice who you are or what's important to you to achieve your mission, of course, but don't let it go the other way either. You can't solve all the world's problems at once. Do the best you can while solving just one, and build from there as you are able.

In My Experience

Standing up and doing something—anything—for all the world to see is scary. And the harder you work on your project, it seems, the more you have to lose. I've been there.

Years ago, I had the idea for this book. I crafted the proposal, developed an outline, wrote some sample chapters, and sent it out to agents and publishers. What if it got rejected? I worried. It did get rejected, and I survived. I sent it out again. What if it got bought? I worried more. Eventually, a publisher did buy it . . . and I panicked.

What started as an abstract concept was suddenly supposed to become a thing. Could I even do it? If I did it, would it be any good? What if people didn't like it? Worse yet, what if people told me they didn't like it? It was almost enough to make me crawl back into my nice warm bed and forget the whole thing. But I didn't.

There were many times when I was working on this book that I thought, I can't do this. Then I'd interview someone like Alex from Project Believe in Me and talk about his venture. I'd get so excited about what he had done and what he was still working on that as soon as I hung up the phone or finished the email, I would dance around the house until I could sit down to write again. If those people could dare so greatly and follow their dreams, then so could I. In fact, knowing they were doing all of these amazing things, I couldn't not try to do something amazing, too.

Change is like that, I think. The more we see other people taking chances, the more willing we are to take a chance ourselves. And so it ripples ever outward.

WHERE DO YOU GO FROM HERE?

So, what can you do with all of this experience you've gained? What's your next step? No matter which direction you decide to go, there's really no end to where these kinds of skills can take you.

First, decide what to do with this venture. Maybe you're ready to embark on a new adventure. If that's the case, you should transition your venture to new leadership, or, if all else fails, shut it down. If you decide to stick with it, you can continue to grow and develop your venture yourself, like Jackie did with Everybody Dance Now! Consider giving yourself an official title that reflects the real work you are doing, such as CEO or executive director. You might even reach a point where your venture brings in enough money to start paying you a salary or passing some of the profits to you as the owner (depending on your tax classification and business structure).

Regardless of what you decide, connecting with other young changemakers like yourself can be very rewarding. Seek out others you admire at events you attend, in groups you belong to, and online. Sharing your common experiences can produce a deeply satisfying bond of friendship and increase your mutual networks.

Perhaps you'd like to check with established organizations you admire to see if they have—or are interested in forming—a youth advisory board. You have a solid track record that proves your commitment to the issue and also shines a light on your abilities.

You may want to get more involved in government through activism, lobbying, youth councils, or even running for a political office. Your awareness of the issues, your public speaking skills, and your networking ability will be useful for all of these opportunities.

The skills you've gained will help you get ahead elsewhere, too. Whether you're heading off to higher education or entering the work force, colleges and companies alike are actively seeking people who have demonstrated problem-solving abilities, leadership experience, and excellent communication skills. Changemaking also shows you are an involved and contributing member of your community, something that is a crucial consideration for hiring managers and college admissions directors. Be sure to include a detailed list of your experiences on all applications and in any interviews you may have so the people evaluating you can see what you've done.

And, of course, you now have all the knowledge and experience you need to start a new organization or business—and be your own boss—now or in the future.

LOOKING FORWARD, AND BACK

However you decide to proceed, remember that you made a real difference. Like those who participated in the big social movements before you, you accomplished something that wouldn't have happened without your unique blend of passion, skills, and caring. You now know you have the power to make the world you want to live in a reality—today, tomorrow, and always—because you started something that mattered. You are a changemaker. And that is one thing that will *never* change.

**UNLESS someone like you cares a whole awful lot,
nothing is going to get better. It's not.**

Dr. Seuss, pseudonym of author and cartoonist
Theodor Seuss Geisel, in *The Lorax*

Acknowledgments

Writing a book is a journey, and the smallest detour can result in a completely different book. In fact, without just the right inspiration, encouragement, and guidance at the perfect time, it might never become a book at all. So it is with heartfelt sincerity that I say this book would not have been possible without the following people.

David Bornstein's *How to Change the World* opened my eyes to the world of social entrepreneurship and started me in a new direction: to bring his message of empowerment and possibility to young people and give them the knowledge needed to start making changes of their own.

David's book also led me to Ashoka, an organization whose vision is an "everyone is a changemaker" world, and to their Youth Venture project, which is aimed at helping young people get started on that path. I'm especially grateful to Jack Knellinger and Jim McGinley from Youth Venture's original Seattle office for being so generous with their time and support in this book's earliest days, and to Gretchen Zucker in Washington DC for providing contacts and support later on. I'm also incredibly honored that the founder of Ashoka himself, Bill Drayton, wrote the foreword.

Melanie Carroll, Zohar Fuller, Karyn Fargo, Danielle Smith, Sarah Gogel, Ines Finchelstein, Romina Laouri Faulb, Marina Mansilla Hermann, Damasia Quesada, Sofia Unanue, and Peter Salomon helped connect me with some of the young people featured in the book. And what a pleasure it was to interview all of those young changemakers. They were my inspiration, and their boundless enthusiasm and amazing achievements kept me going when things got tough. I can't thank them enough for giving up their precious time to answer all my questions!

The Society of Children's Book Writers and Illustrators (SCBWI) was an ever-present network providing both knowledge and camaraderie, especially Joni Sensel and Kim Baker. SCBWI also led me to my talented critique group: Kevan Atteberry, Lois Brandt, Susan Greenway, Curtis Manley, Jeanie Mebane, Dan Richards, Dana Sullivan, and Arlene Williams. Their thoughtful feedback and support is always much appreciated.

I had the good fortune of getting input on this manuscript from several editors, too. Thank you to Nicole Geiger, Ali McCart, and Lindsay Brown for their expert guidance.

Every single day I feel blessed to be a part of the creative, generous family that is Erin Murphy Literary Agency. In particular, the fine debut authors I've been fortunate enough to blog with at EMu's Debuts have been wonderful resources and great friends throughout this entire process. And words really can't express the depth of my gratitude for my fantastic agent, Ammi-Joan Paquette!

My family's do-it-yourself attitude, compassion, and integrity have made me who I am and allowed me to make this book what it is. I thank them from the bottom of my heart—especially my husband, Bernie, and our two children—for their ongoing influence and support.

I know there are people whose names I've left out and others I'll probably never know. I'm grateful to each of them for their contributions, no matter how big or small. I literally couldn't have done it without them.

And, of course, what is a book without a reader? Thank you!

I will donate 10 percent of my proceeds from sales of this book to Ashoka's Youth Venture to support their mission of empowering young people to begin a lifelong path of changemaking.

Please join the conversation, ask questions, and share your changemaking experience at be-a-changemaker.com!

Resources

There are a lot more resources beyond this book that can help you launch and manage your venture successfully. Here are a few that I've found to be especially helpful. Check them out for yourself, and stay on the lookout for new and improved resources, too!

PROFILED WEBSITES

- Chapter 1, Free the Children: www.freethechildren.org

- Chapter 4, Project ORANGS: projectorangs.org

- Chapter 5, Richard's Rwanda: www.richardsrwanda.org

- Chapter 6, Greening Forward: greeningforward.org

- Chapter 8, Transition House: awearness-yac.tumblr.com

- Chapter 9, Youth Ultimate Project: www.youthultimateproject.org

- Chapter 10, Les Manos United: https://www.facebook.com/LES.MANOS.UNITED

- Chapter 12, StudentRND: studentrnd.org

- Chapter 14, TEDxRedmond: tedxredmond.com

- Chapter 15, Change the World Kids: www.changetheworldkids.org

- Chapter 16, NeverSeconds: neverseconds.blogspot.com

- Chapter 17, Everybody Dance Now: everybodydancenow.org

- Chapter 18, Project Believe in Me: projectbelieveinme.org

WEBSITES

The internet makes it easy to connect with other young people who have big ideas—and to access resources to help you make those ideas a reality. These are some of the websites I found to be good resources for young people and for businesspeople in general. Each is accompanied by a description, most often in the organization's own words.

BY OR FOR YOUTH

- The Giraffe Heroes Project: "EnCouraging Today's Heroes-Training Tomorrow's." giraffe.org

- Junior Achievement: "Junior Achievement teaches students how to succeed in a global economy." studentcenter.ja.org

- RandomKid: "The RandomKid mission is to provide staff and services to youth, of all backgrounds and abilities, for the development, management, and accomplishment of their goals to help others." randomkid.org

- SAGE Global: "SAGE Global is an international nonprofit corporation dedicated to teenage entrepreneurs." sageglobal.org

- TakingITGlobal: "TakingITGlobal is one of the world's leading networks of young people learning about, engaging with, and working towards tackling global challenges." www.tigweb.org

- Young Entrepreneur: *Entrepreneur* magazine is a well-known resource for businesspeople of all kinds, and this page on the website is geared toward young entrepreneurs. youngentrepreneur.com

- Young Social Innovators: "Promoting and leading the way in education for social innovation in Ireland, Young Social Innovators encourages, motivates and creates new opportunities for young people to actively participate in the world around them." youngsocialinnovators.ie

- YouthActionNet: "YouthActionNet invests in the power and promise of young social entrepreneurs around the globe." youthactionnet.org

GENERAL BUSINESS TIPS

- 99U: "At 99U, we deliver the action-oriented insights that you didn't get in school, highlighting real-world best practices for making ideas happen." 99u.com

- Entrepreneurship.org: "This site provides innovative educational tools, informative channels covering the latest issues and insights affecting entrepreneurs, and a popular events section that gives entrepreneurs an opportunity to connect." entrepreneurship.org

- Mind Tools: "We believe that anyone can learn and use these simple processes and techniques to make the very most of their careers." mindtools.com

- Startups for Social Entrepreneurs Program: This college program helps students "discover how to put your passion and energy to work making the world a better place." www.straighterline.com/landing/startups-for-social-entrepreneurs

BOOKS

Books are, of course, an amazing resource. Some of them show us *how* to do things, and others inspire us by sharing the stories of how other people accomplished their goals.

BY OR FOR YOUTH

- *The 7 Habits of Highly Effective Teens: the Ultimate Teenage Success Guide* by Sean Covey

- *Better than a Lemonade Stand!: Small Business Ideas for Kids* by Daryl Bernstein

- *Chill: Stress-Reducing Techniques for a More Balanced, Peaceful You* by Deborah Reber

- *"Cool Stuff" They Should Teach in School: Cruise into the Real World . . . with Styyyyle* by Kent Healy and Kyle Healy

- *Free the Children: A Young Man Fights Against Child Labor and Proves That Children Can Change the World* by Craig Kielburger with Kevin Major

- *How To Guide to Starting an Earth Savers Club: An Environmental Leadership Resource for Youth by Youth* by Charles Orgbon

- *It's Our World, Too!: Young People Who Are Making a Difference: How They Do It —How You Can, Too!* by Phillip M. Hoose

- *It's Up to Us: Making a Difference in a Challenging World* by John Graham

- *It's Your World—If You Don't Like It, Change It: Activism for Teenagers* by Mikki Halpin

- *The Kid's Guide to Social Action: How to Solve the Social Problems You Choose—and Turn Creative Thinking into Positive Action* by Barbara Lewis

- *Kids with Courage: True Stories about Young People Making a Difference* by Barbara Lewis

- *Me to We: Finding Meaning in a Material World* by Craig Kielburger and Marc Kielburger

- *NeverSeconds: The Incredible Story of Martha Payne* by Martha Payne and David Payne

- *A Random Book about the Power of Anyone* by Talia Leman

- *Start It Up: The Complete Teen Business Guide to Turning Your Passions into Pay* by Kenrya Rankin

- *The Success Principles for Teens: How to Get From Where You Are to Where You Want to Be* by Jack Canfield and Kent Healy

- *Voices of Hope (Heroes' Stories for Challenging Times)* by Ann Medlock

- *The Young Entrepreneur's Guide to Starting and Running a Business* by Steve Mariotti

CHANGEMAKING AND SOCIAL ENTREPRENEURSHIP

- *Do Good Well: Your Guide to Leadership, Action, and Social Innovation* by Nina Vasan and Jennifer Przybylo

- *Do It Anyway: The New Generation of Activists* by Courtney E. Martin

- *The Generosity Plan: Sharing Your Time, Treasure, and Talent to Shape the World* by Kathy LeMay

- *How to Change the World: Social Entrepreneurs and the Power of New Ideas* by David Bornstein

- *Join the Club: How Peer Pressure Can Transform the World* by Tina Rosenberg

- *The Power of Unreasonable People: How Social Entrepreneurs Create Markets That Change the World* by John Elkington and Pamela Hartigan

- *The Real Problem Solvers: Social Entrepreneurs in America,* edited by Ruth A. Shapiro

- *Rippling: How Social Entrepreneurs Spread Innovation Throughout the World* by Beverly Schwartz

- *The Social Entrepreneur's Handbook: How to Start, Build, and Run a Business That Improves the World* by Rupert Scofield

- *The Social Entrepreneur's Playbook: Pressure Test, Plan, Launch and Scale Your Enterprise* by Ian C. MacMillan and James D. Thompson

- *Social Entrepreneurship: What Everyone Needs to Know* by David Bornstein and Susan Davis

- *The Solution Revolution: How Business, Government, and Social Enterprises Are Teaming Up to Solve Society's Toughest Problems* by William D. Eggers and Paul Macmillan

- *Start Something that Matters* by Blake Mycoskie

- *Stick Your Neck Out: A Street-Smart Guide to Creating Change in Your Community and Beyond* by John Graham

GENERAL BUSINESS TIPS

- *Behind Closed Doors: Secrets of Great Management* by Johanna Rothman and Esther Derby

- *The Corner Office: Indispensable and Unexpected Lessons from CEOs on How to Lead and Succeed* by Adam Bryant

- *The Education of Millionaires: It's Not What You Think and It's Not Too Late* by Michael Ellsberg

- *Presenting to Win: The Art of Telling Your Story* by Jerry Weissman

- *Start with Why: How Great Leaders Inspire Everyone to Take Action* by Simon Sinek

MOVIES AND TELEVISION SHOWS

These documentaries tell the stories of some amazing people and their drive to do good in the world.

- *Emmanuel's Gift* documents how Emmanuel Ofosu Yeboah, who was born with a severely deformed leg, is working to support disabled people in his homeland of Ghana and worldwide.

- *Jiro Dreams of Sushi* provides an inside look at how this sushi chef has used his passion to start—and maintain—a world-renowned restaurant.

- *The New Heroes* chronicles the stories of fourteen social entrepreneurs around the world.